OTCH DREAMS

The Agony and the Ecstasy of Life with Competition Obedience Dogs

Willard Bailey

Author of *Remembering to Breathe: Inside Dog Obedience Competition*

Two books in one! *The Last Days of Honeybear* and *Such a Little Spirit!*

Copyright © 2007 by Willard Bailey

ISBN 0-7414-3989-1

Published by:

PUBLISHING.COM

1094 New DeHaven Street, Suite 100
West Conshohocken, PA 19428-2713
Info@buybooksontheweb.com
www.buybooksontheweb.com
Toll-free (877) BUY BOOK
Local Phone (610) 941-9999
Fax (610) 941-9959

Printed in the United States of America

Printed on Recycled Paper

Published April 2007

For Barbara, who has been at the center of my world for more than half a century.

■ PREFACE ■

Before you begin this book, have you read *Remembering to Breathe: Inside Dog Obedience Competition?* What follows — particularly Book One, *The Last Days of Honeybear* — is a sequel to *Remembering to Breathe.* If you read *Remembering to Breathe* first, you'll have the background, know the characters, appreciate the nuances ... enjoy *OTCH Dreams* much more.

Remembering to Breathe was published by Infinity Publishing. The quickest way to obtain that book is to order direct from the publisher. Online: *www.buybooksontheweb.com.* By phone: 1-877-289-2665.

If you can't wait, if *OTCH Dreams* is screaming to be read, here's a little help — thumbnail bios of a few of the central characters.

- *Barbara* My long-suffering wife who got me a golden retriever puppy for Christmas in 1989 and has gone on to endure (often cheerfully) countless cold, dark mornings in far-flung outposts of the obedience trial circuit; tens of thousands of boring, grinding miles to and from those outposts; helping to lug, collectively, tons of stuff in and out of hundreds of shows and matches; a tsunami of training paraphernalia ... everywhere; and dog hair in the soup.

- *Bebop* My first border collie. A son of the all-time United States border collie herding trial champion, Nick. My OTCH-dog-to-be. My future Gaines Super Dog. You'll become intimately acquainted with Bebop in Book Two, *Such A Little Spirit!*
- *Cheddar* My second golden retriever. A son of Mike MacDonald's SixPak, the eighth-ranked obedience competition dog of all time. Cheddar is officially known to the American Kennel Club as One Ash the Cheese UD.
- *Debby Boehm* The instructor, and ultimately close friend, who encountered Honeybear and me when I was still trying to figure out which end of the leash you attach to the dog. Debby sees all, misses nothing and has been central to any success we've had.
- *Skippy* and *Honeybear* Well, it took an entire book *(Remembering to Breathe)* to tell our story and to recount the life-defining adventure we shared. Here you're on your own.

In any case, enjoy!

W.B.

■ *Book One* ■

THE LAST DAYS OF HONEYBEAR

■ CHAPTER 1 ■

It Ain't Over 'Til It's Over

When last we encountered Honeybear (HB), she was having the time of her life. And so was I (*Remembering to Breathe: Inside Dog Obedience Competition*, Chapter 57).

On the day Honeybear finished her OTCH at 9 years, 9 months and 25 days, I promised her she'd never have to jump again. The final 11 points had been a tough go.

First the ruptured anterior cruciate ligament, repaired with a tibial plateau-leveling osteotomy. It made her right hind leg stronger than it had ever been, but it cost us six months. Quite a layoff for a canine athlete who's bearing down on ten years of age.

Then her left hip, diagnosed as mildly dysplastic when she was 14 months old, finally began to bother her. Several times in practice she refused to jump. Acupuncture treatments may have helped. Or maybe it was the power of adrenaline. Or even the potency of the bloodsweat that gushed from my every pore as I watched, petrified, each time HB approached a jump. In any case, she never refused a jump in a trial. Meanwhile, all her other activities were normal — running, heeling, playing ball, begging at the kitchen counter.

But enough was enough. And October 17, 1999, the day she finished her OTCH in Las Cruces, New Mexico, was the last time she competed in a regulation class.

Nevertheless, HB was not cut out to be a couch potato. None of my dogs are. From the moment I carry them into the house at seven weeks of age, training is a major part of their lives. And they love it. Why snatch that away from them the day they retire from regulation competition?

And exactly what was I supposed to do with Honeybear when it was time to go to the park for Bebop's training sessions? Leave her standing behind the door? Stoic. Knowing where we were going, and knowing she was being left behind.

Or picture this. It's time to train Bebop. HB goes along in the van. We pull up to the large grassy area that used to be hers. I set up a ring. Honeybear knows every inch of that ring. She knows those jumps and the bags they come out of. Then I begin to train Bebop. Honeybear hears my commands and wants to respond. But all she can do is press her nose against the van window and eat her heart out.

No, that wasn't how it was going to be. The only part of HB's game that had deteriorated was jumping. She couldn't do that anymore, but I wasn't going to relegate her to the couch. That, I was sure, would cause her to die of a broken heart.

Long before Honeybear had finished her OTCH, I had decided to keep her plenty active in her retirement. The focal point of that activity would be Veterans obedience, a nonregular class offered at most AKC obedience club trials and a few all-breed dog shows.

No jumping would be required. In fact, the Veterans class exercises are the Novice exercises. A dog must be seven or older to compete in Veterans.

Well, I reasoned, *if we're going into the ring, we might as well win*. And that meant we'd have to practice. Whenever Bebop would train, HB would train, too. A little heeling, a recall, a stand for exam ... and lots of ballplaying. No pressure, lots of play. And the best part about it, that old white face would still be at my side.

So the plan was that from time to time we'd show in Veterans. No big deal. I had no idea it would evolve into a second competition career for Honeybear.

I entered her in Veterans here and there. If there was a match, I'd enter her in Novice — exactly the same ring routine. I thought she'd do well, but her performances snapped my head back. Right from the start, we knocked off scores of 198, 198, 199.5, 199, 198.5. When we stepped forward to accept our first-place ribbons, I'd say, "Honeybear, where were those scores in Novice A?" Of course, we had some "bad" runs, too: 197 and 197.5.

When it was ring time, she'd burst out of her crate or out of the van, often with a joyous whoop. Never before in our obedience career had either of us had such a consistently wonderful time.

As HB's second career took off like it was shot from a gun, others began to notice. Locally, the entry in Veterans classes swelled, often to eight or nine dogs. It was obvious some were taking it as seriously as we were and had done at least a modicum of training before they showed up in the ring. Others, well, that was obvious, too. Their dogs had been dragged off the couch that morning and would go right back up there at the end of the day.

During 2000, we ran off a string of 11 straight firsts in Veterans, averaging 198.6.

About to award ribbons following the Veterans class at Vegas Valley Dog Obedience Club's trial in October 2000, Judge Pauline Andrus told the spectators assembled outside the ring, "This class is where you see the really great dogs — they're all retired."

Of course, she was right. By and large, the dogs who had dragged through their careers, who had hated it because they

Photo: Bill Kohler & Associates

Honeybear

had been taught to hate it, who along with their handlers had had enough, were home on the couch.

But those who had been brought along in such a way that they loved to train, loved to show, couldn't wait to get out there, were often excellent in the Veterans ring at a ripe old age. And their owners, moist-eyed and bursting with pride, couldn't wait to get into the ring with them ... perhaps just one more time.

My own moist eyes would come during the long sit when I had time to contemplate that old white face — all those old white faces lined up across the ring. I'd stand there and say to myself, *How many times, Honeybear ... ? How many times across more than a decade of Open competition have I returned to the ring to find you sitting there just like this, so straight, so true?*

I became an evangelistic advocate for keeping older dogs active. So you can imagine my dismay when, in August of 2000, at the very time when HB was on a roll, Pat Krause, American Kennel Club assistant vice president for companion dog events, showed up in Arizona for an AKC seminar and proposed elimination of the Veterans class as we know it.

Shortly after lunch, Pat stepped to the microphone and began with, "Now I want to share with you something that's very near and dear to my heart." She went on to say she'd like to eliminate Veterans as a nonregular class. Eliminate the competition, eliminate the awarding of the ribbons, eliminate the old dogs' chance to shine, to hear the applause, perhaps to recall the glory days. Instead she proposed a "parade of champions, titleholders," whatever.

I could not believe what I was hearing. And it was coming from the mouth of the person who was in a position to indeed scuttle the Veterans class. It was an example of what can happen when a person in a position of power gets a bad idea, then falls in love with it ("… something that's very near and dear to my heart.")

When she was finished, she asked for questions, comments. I raised my hand. When she recognized me, I stood up. "*That is one of the worst ideas I've ever heard,*" I began. Then I went from there.

A few days after the seminar, I followed up with a letter which said, in part:

> *You are suggesting I drag my older dog out of the backyard or off the couch, where he's been vegetating, and occasionally bring him to a blow-off class where no skills are required.*
>
> *I'm convinced a good competition dog knows the difference between serious training and just fooling around. I'm also convinced that dog knows the difference between a good performance and a sloppy appearance in the ring.*
>
> *If you take an older dog out and regularly do consistent, serious training … if you challenge that dog physically, at a level compatible with his physical capabilities … if you challenge him mentally, that dog is going to be happier, healthier and live longer.*
>
> *I believe you and the AKC would agree, we should all be encouraging training methodologies which produce obedience competition dogs who are fast, accurate and above all love to train and compete. If the latter is the case, the dog will be happier the longer he can train and compete (to the level of his capabilities).*
>
> *Therefore, if you create events which serve as incentives for competition handlers to challenge their wonderful old dogs physically and mentally, you've done a life-enriching service for those dogs.*

> *On the other hand, to relegate them to a "parade*
> *of champions" would be a disservice.*

As has been the experience of so many of us in dealing with the AKC, I received no response. Fortunately, though, that was the last anyone heard of the "near-and-dear-to-my-heart" idea.

Meanwhile, Honeybear was storming through her appearances in the Veterans ring. For almost all of her second career, she averaged a few tenths of a point above 198. It was as if she had thought it was all over, then suddenly her career was reborn and she was savoring every precious moment of it.

Nearly every day she was out training again, frolicking at my side, eyes shining through advancing cataracts, old rear end dancing, albeit stiffly.

In the ring, she was mowing 'em down — first place after first place after first place after … whoops! On November 5, 2000, at the Old Pueblo Dog Training Club's trial in Tucson, she had almost completed another near-perfect run when we got to the recall exercise. She was almost to front when I saw a confused look in her eyes. Then she swung halfway into an automatic finish and sat there looking guilty. That little caper brought us our first second-place finish in Veterans competition.

Twelve days later, at the specialty show of the Palo Verde Golden Retriever Club (Tucson), she replicated that stunt and again we finished second. After that, the problem vanished as inexplicably as it had come, and we were off and running again — wall-to-wall firsts for the next 15 months.

Honeybear experienced only one truly bad weekend during her Veterans career. That was the weekend of the Phoenix Field and Obedience Club trials, February 22 and 23, 2003.

On Saturday morning we were beaten fair and square by a bichon frisé and her handler who simply outheeled us. That defeat was notable because it marked the only time in Veterans competition that HB was beaten by another dog. Every other time she failed to finish first — and there were only three — she beat herself. Including the next morning.

During the group exercises, she rose to greet me each time I returned to her. Why? I have no idea what was going on in that fuzzy yellow head that morning. She had never done it before, and she never did it again. That weekend marked the final time HB failed to finish first.

Four days later, at the Valle del Sol Golden Retriever Club's fall specialty, it was "Honeybear weather." It had rained for several days and the polo field at WestWorld of Scottsdale was soggy at best. And "at best" did not apply to our obedience ring. By the time Veterans began, the regular classes had been held and the surface had been trampled into squishy mud with standing water in several spots. Then, just as HB and I were about to enter the ring, another downpour began.

Indeed it was Honeybear weather, and HB frisked through it to win the class with a 197. Then we tore back to our van where a Bonz awaited.

Well into her 14th year she was still having the time of her life. And as long as she was lovin' it, we'd keep going.

I entered us in the specialty show of the Golden Retriever Club of Los Angeles, to be held at San Juan Capistrano on May 10.

The judge for the specialty obedience classes was Curtis Cunningham. Across HB's long obedience career, we had shown under him several times. HB had gotten her second CDX leg in his ring, winning the Open A class with a 194.5. Now, on a sunny May morning in Southern California, she was two points better than that, winning the Veterans class with a 196.5.

As Judge Cunningham prepared to hand out ribbons to the top four finishers, all of whom had scored in the 190s, he told the spectators, "Look at these old dogs! Can you image what they must have been like in their prime?"

All of which was very nice. But I was seeing something else. HB had been slightly laggy that morning. And her 196.5, while best in the class, was at least a point and a half below the 198-plus scores she had been knocking off regularly the past three years. Only recently had her average dipped slightly below 198.

As we left the ring that morning, I was carrying our first-place ribbon as well as the one presented to the highest scoring dog in nonregular classes. Honeybear had won everything that was available to be won. I was so proud.

My big girl was still giving her best, but now she was laboring to do it. That beautiful spring morning in Southern California would be her final time in competition. She would go out on top, the way I wanted all of us to remember her.

It had been quite a second career. HB had shown in Veterans 28 times. She had won the class 24 times, finished second 3 times, bombed once.

Her retirement from competition in no way implied couch potato status. As always, when Bebop and Cheddar trained, Honeybear trained … lightly, gently.

We'd heel with treats. She'd do scent articles, joyously. She'd do go-outs, turn, sit, get a treat. She'd retrieve her dumbbell and return with her head high, her tail going furiously.

My decision to retire her was reinforced in a potent way later that summer. Old Pueblo Dog Training Club held classes and ring run-throughs on Friday evenings at Reid Park in Tucson. Cheddar was a year old and coming along well. I wanted him to get used to the simulated show atmosphere. And it was a chance to let Bebop and Honeybear participate in a limited way.

So once in a while on Friday afternoons we'd pack a lunch, pile everyone into the van and set out for Tucson. I'd take Cheddar and Honeybear into the Novice ring and let Bebop tear around like a maniac in Utility.

On a Friday evening in September, I set HB up in a line of dogs for Novice sits and downs. On the judge's command, I left her on a long sit. I hadn't gone 15 feet when I heard the judge say, "Honeybear's down." Impossible! HB hadn't blown a sit or a down for at least six years. Nevertheless, I turned around and there she was, lying down, looking guilty. I put her back up, but she managed to go down two more times during the one minute sit.

How can this be? I thought. It had been 12½ years since our near-catastrophic siege with broken sits and downs in Novice A. Since then, HB had been the most solid stays dog I had ever known. I had watched some of America's best handlers agonize over broken stays. Dick Guetzloff, one of the greatest of them all, liked to tell people, "There are only two kinds of dogs, those that have a stays problem and those that are *going* to have a stays problem."

Now this! It didn't take a veterinarian to tell me what was wrong. Sitting hurt. So we wouldn't do that anymore. Honeybear's range of activities was narrowing.

■ CHAPTER 2 ■

Reality Hits

In the summer of 1972, Barbara and I vacationed in Nassau, Bahamas. It rained all week. But I didn't care. I was in our hotel room transfixed, spellbound by a book, *The Boys of Summer*. In it, Roger Kahn chronicled his visits, some two decades after they retired from baseball, with members of one of the most exciting teams ever to take the field, the Brooklyn Dodgers of the 1950s. *The Boys of Summer,* at its heart, was about time and what it does to strong men.

Although a third of a century has passed, *The Boys of Summer* remains the one read that has had the greatest impact on my life and my writing.

Kahn had journeyed about America, visiting with the likes of Jackie Robinson, Carl Erskine, Duke Snider, Pee Wee Reese, Billy Cox, Roy Campanella, and Carl Furillo — now long past their youth and sinew. In the fall of 1970, he had dropped in on Elwin C. "Preacher" Roe, the crafty left-hander who, across the decade of the '50s, won 93 games for the Dodgers and pitched brilliantly in three World Series.

In his glory days, as he stood on the mound facing the opposition, Roe, in Kahn's words, "was all bones and angles, even to a pointed nose and a sharp chin." Now, at 55, as they sat on a bank at the side of a country road in the Ozarks and looked across the overgrown field where he had played baseball as a boy, Roe was portly, wore glasses and had grown jowls.

"Can you imagine startin' here and getting to pitch for the championship of the World Series in New York City?" Roe asked Kahn, shaking his head in wonder.

"Can *you* imagine it?" Kahn asked. "Can you make it come alive?"

"All of it," Preacher said, "One thing makes a feller sad is knowin' that's behind, and what's wrong with him is nothing that giving back twenty years wouldn't cure. 'Cept they don't do that, do they?"

■ ■ ■

Fast forward now, 28 years.

Honeybear turned 11 on December 22, 2000. I took her to Wendy's for a hamburger for her birthday. If memory serves me right, it was only the third hamburger of her life.

Her first was won by virtue of perfect execution of her best exercise at an obedience trial, the sandwich grab. We were at the 1994 Superstition Kennel Club shows. We had competed in Open B and our 196.5 had been good for fourth place.

Afterwards we went for a walk. We had meandered past the vendors' stands and were threading our way through the congestion around the breed rings when I felt a quick tug on the leash. Like the momentary tension one feels when a large fish hits the bait.

I didn't catch so much as a glimpse of the guy's cheeseburger. It had been atop a paper plate on a chair beside him. HB saw it, grabbed it and wolfed it down. All in a split second.

The man who had been preparing to enjoy the sandwich sat in stunned silence for a moment.

"What was on that plate?" I asked.

"A cheeseburger," he replied and began to laugh.

"Oh, I'm so sorry," I stammered, "I'll get you another one."

"No, no, no," he protested. "If she'll just give me a kiss, that will be enough." Honeybear was happy to oblige with a big, slurpy smacker ... or five.

Barbara brought home HB's second hamburger — just beef and bun, nothing on it — from Wendy's in October of 1999, in celebration of her OTCH.

So on the day HB turned 11, she got a hamburger and lots of extra attention. But I didn't consider the day a happy occasion. That was the year reality hit me. I wonder how many times that day I hammered my emotions with, *But I don't want her to be 11. I want her to be four again. I want her to be out on the polo field with me again, running and jumping and playing and learning new things.*

Then, early in 2001, there was the wrenching episode about her ears.

Honeybear produced a lot of wax and was prone to ear infections. To keep the situation under control, we cleaned her ears twice a week, on Wednesday and Saturday mornings. On those mornings, ear cleaning was added to the coat brushing and teeth cleaning routine.

I had watched others — Chuck Toben, our veterinarian, and Tracy Riendeau, a veterinary technician — clean HB's ears, and they made it look like a piece of cake. But somehow the dexterity required eluded me, and at our house ear cleaning was a two-person job.

The undertaking went like this: Honeybear was on the grooming table. I held her head steady while Barbara lifted the flap of one ear and, using an eyedropper, put five to seven drops of Epi-Otic, an ear-cleansing solution, into the ear. Then Barbara massaged the ear canal from the base upward for about 10 seconds, driving wax and detritus upward in the canal.

Then we changed places. I twisted a dry cotton ball so that it had a point ... well, in the beginning it did. While Barbara held HB's head steady, I inserted the cotton into the ear canal and, turning it like a corkscrew, did my darndest to get out any wax that may have accumulated in there.

I was lousy at that. Several times when he had to deal with accumulated wax in HB's ears, Dr. Toben said, "Willard, be more aggressive when you do this." The problem was the cotton ball would wad up, and the point that I had carefully constructed would flatten. I'd end up corkscrewing like crazy, but the now-blunt cotton would penetrate only about a quarter of an inch into the ear canal.

The operation, modestly successful as it was, required two people, largely because Honeybear loved Epi-Otic. When I was finished, before I'd wash my hands, she'd have it no other way but that she be allowed to lick my fingers. If I moved to retreat, she'd lean so far she'd plunge off the table.

So for better or for worse it was a two-person operation.

In February of 2001, as Honeybear was cruising all too quickly through her 12th year, Barbara was going to have to be out of town for a week. Which would leave HB and me flying solo at ear-cleaning time.

We were in the bathroom one morning. Barbara was putting on makeup. I was about to brush my teeth.

"Oh Lord," I said, "I'm going to have to do Honeybear's ears twice while you're gone."

Barbara shook her head in mock disgust. "She's an obedience dog," she said, "an Obedience Trial Champion. All you have to do is train her. Teach her to hold her head still." There was silence for a moment. Then, warming to her little put-on, she added, "Teach her the commands. 'Straight' means hold her nose straight forward, she mustn't turn her head. Say 'Lift!' and her earflap stands straight up."

At which point I beat it out of there as fast as I could, eyes brimming with tears. Barbara never knew that each time she had said, "teach her," the words had cut through me like a knife.

I'll never forget January 5, 1992, the day Honeybear finished her Companion Dog title at the Kennel Club of Palm Springs show in Indio, California. As we drove home along I-10 that afternoon, I was ecstatic. Happier than I had been before in my life. My first obedience competition dog had finished her first title, and it hadn't been easy.

Well beyond that, all the way home I kept saying, "Now I get to teach her the Open exercises. Now I get to teach her so many new things." We'd be on the polo field, just the two of us. She'd be learning and her tail would be going like crazy.

Now, in her 12th year, I wished to God that she were three or four again so I could teach her lots of new things. And she could learn with tail-wagging exuberance. And it would be the purest of all joy for both of us. And I could savor every moment.

Yes, one thing makes a feller sad is knowin' that's behind, and what's wrong is nothing that giving back eight years wouldn't cure. 'Cept they don't do that, do they?

■ CHAPTER 3 ■

The Slippery Slope

You watch your furry old friends deteriorate and it breaks your heart, one little piece at a time. You see their eyes get cloudier and cloudier. And yet those old eyes still somehow manage to sparkle when the dog is happy.

One day it dawns on you that your friend isn't hearing so well. It gets worse and worse. She dozes through kitchen sounds that used to bring her running. Nevertheless, she still arrives promptly and waggly tailed at mealtime, less because she hears the food canister opening, more because of the context in which it occurs. And it reaches a point where those hand signals you taught her for Utility become a vital part of everyday life. In fact, across Honeybear's final 15 months in the Veterans ring, I had used hand signals exclusively, no verbals.

Here in Arizona, we have lots of tile flooring. That's where we first notice an old dog's back end is beginning to give out. In the beginning, the dog has just-noticeable difficulty getting up off the floor. It's most difficult when she's been lying down a while. As time passes, it gets worse, more and more of a struggle. That became my barometer with Honeybear.

Sometime in 2003 I said to Dr. Toben, "Honeybear's on the slippery slope." He nodded affirmatively. "I'll tell you right now," I continued, "when she goes, it's going to be her back end."

I knew that someday she was going to get down and not be able to get back up. That would be decision time. And I knew what that decision would have to be. I had come to grips with the euthanasia dilemma a long time ago.

That wrenching decision becomes imperative as an animal you love slips into a state of being where her quality of life is lousy. It demands gut-level answers to two basic questions: "Whose needs are we meeting here?" And, "Is it about what's best for the dog, or is it all about *me*?" Most of all, at the root of it, it's about courage versus cowardice.

The statement, "I just want to keep her a little while longer," is self-serving and often leads to animal abuse. So does desperation surgery — to "fix" the unfixable or to "find out what's going on in there" — when the handwriting is clearly on the wall. Dr. Toben told me, "Most of my clients need answers." Yeah, right. At the animal's expense.

Then there's, "Oh I love her so much I can't bring myself to take her over there (to the veterinarian's office to be put to sleep)." That's gutlessness. Not enough intestinal fortitude to do the right thing for a dear friend who has given you her all for a lifetime ... and trusts you.

The decision to put a beloved animal to sleep is the most painful one to carry out that I've experienced in my lifetime. The answer is: Just do it! It doesn't matter how much it hurts me. My feelings aren't the issue here. We're talking about selfless compassion versus spineless self-indulgence.

How people respond to the needs of their animals as the end nears is, I strongly believe, a litmus test of their compassion, their courage, the depth of their character, their inner strength.

When we arrived in Phoenix, I met, through professional circles, a guy we'll call Stan Shultz. He was in charge of fund-raising for a huge multihospital system in Arizona. Stan was the consummate politician; glad-handing was the foundation of his game. *Scratch the surface,* I thought, *and you'll find there isn't much substance there.* So I tolerated him, that's all.

In the '90s I had an important client in southeastern Arizona, Tucson Medical Center Foundation. For 13 years, the foundation ran an annual event called the Greater Issues Series. Each year's affair was an elaborate dinner featuring an internationally prominent speaker. Across the years, the foundation presented luminaries ranging from former secretary of state Henry Kissinger to war correspondent Peter Arnet, columnist and Pulitzer Prize winner George F. Will to former national security advisor and ambassador to the United Nations Jean Kirkpatrick.

In the fall of 1996, Simon Peres, former prime minister of Israel, was the attraction. The purpose of the annual event was "friendraising" for the foundation. And due to intense interest in Middle East tensions, the several hundred attendees were a who's who of the movers and shakers from Tucson and much of Arizona.

As a consultant to the foundation, I considered it de rigueur that I support such efforts. So I ponied up a bundle and drove to Tucson for the dinner.

During the cocktail reception, I was struck by two things.

First, the place was crawling with American and Israeli secret service agents. And I could have sworn they were all watching me.

Second, Stan Shultz, sensing a splendid opportunity to brown-nose, was also in attendance (at his organization's expense) and vigorously working the room.

Eventually we were tossed together in the sea of dignitaries and secret service agents. By and by the conversation turned to dogs. Stan told me that only yesterday his family had lost their longtime canine member. The dog had come to them as a puppy and been part of the family for nearly 15 years.

"But he was getting old," Stan told me matter-of-factly, "and I figured it was time to have him put to sleep. So yesterday I dropped him off at the Humane Society."

What a gutless way to handle the passing of a dear old friend!

I don't remember what kind of rubber chicken we had for dinner that evening. I couldn't tell you one thing Simon Peres had to say. But I sure remember the words of Stan Shultz as he validated the assessment I had made years earlier: characterwise, there was simply nothing there.

A neighbor — we'll call her Brenda — had a miniature schnauzer, Sasha. In time, the years caught up with Sasha. She was blind, deaf and could no longer control her bowels or bladder.

I'd see Brenda on the street. "I know I should have Sasha put to sleep," she'd lament, "but I just can't bring myself to take her over there."

"Brenda," I'd say, trying not to show my anger, "you've got to pull yourself together and do what's right for Sasha." Which fell on deaf ears.

Sasha spent the last weeks of her life isolated from her family, penned up in a utility room, peeing and pooping on the tile floor, bumbling into the walls, the washer and dryer, and the makeshift gate that confined her.

How can that be regarded as anything short of dog abuse?

And then there was Marlene and her sheltie, Ginger. They showed in obedience competition and did well in spite of the fact that Ginger had been severely coddled all her life. It's the same with every dog Marlene trains. They know all the exercises. What they don't know is how to function in the world.

Nevertheless, Ginger was making slow progress toward an OTCH when she began having persistent diarrhea. Metronidazole would stop the flow for a while, then it would start up again — a cycle that was repeated many times for a year. All the while, veterinarians pressed Marlene to do more extensive diagnostic tests. But Marlene procrastinated, coming up with various rationalizations why not. It was clear to those who were close to her that she was afraid of what she might learn.

Finally, Ginger, losing weight and becoming weak, could no longer participate in obedience trials. She couldn't even practice the exercises at home. On the day Ginger collapsed, Marlene rushed her in for exploratory surgery. It was no surprise when the surgeon found that the dog's organs were riddled with cancer. "It would be best if we didn't bring her out of the anesthetic," he advised.

"No," Marlene said, "I don't want Ginger to die in some veterinarian's office."

So they closed Ginger's abdomen and Marlene took her home. At which point the vigil commenced. For weeks Marlene isolated herself with Ginger in a bedroom. Mostly, Marlene's contacts with the real world were limited to phone conversations with friends — often a rambling hour or more in length.

"I just want to keep her a little while longer," she told me. Then rushed to assure me, "She's not suffering!"

What I wanted to do was drive over there, grab her by the shoulders, shake her and bellow in her face. Instead, I tried in the gentlest manner I could muster. "Marlene," I said, "what you need to do is look in the mirror and ask yourself, 'Whose needs am I meeting?'" Predictably, that accomplished nothing.

Eventually, Marlene went on the Internet and searched until she found out how she could euthanize the dog at home with pills. Then she acquired a large bottle from a vet who was a friend.

"I don't want her in the hands of any third party," she told me. *Better,* I thought, *that the dog suffer at your hands than go peacefully and in a timely manner in the hands of someone who knows what they're doing.*

Finally, after the pathetic saga had dragged on for weeks at the dog's expense, Marlene put the pills down Ginger's throat, one by gagging one, in sufficient quantity that Ginger finally succumbed.

Well, there'd be none of that here. Honeybear had given me her all — performancewise and affectionwise — for a lifetime. The day would come when I'd be compelled by intense love to suck it up and do what would be best for *her*.

■ ■ ■

Our animals have been treated at Apollo Animal Hospital for 20 years. Dr. Toben has been our go-to guy for 18 of those years. Each doctor has his own examining room. Which means I've been in Dr. Toben's room a zillion times — with three cats, two poodles, two goldens, two border collies, and a Sheltie.

After the animal is weighed, I'm led into that room by a receptionist who says, "Dr. Toben will be with you shortly." Then the door is closed and I'm alone with my furry friend and my thoughts.

How many times have I sat there with Honeybear, looked at that examining table and thought, *"Well, HB, that's where you'll die"*?

Until … until when? I'm not sure. But at some point the thought of my best friends dying on a cold table in the alien, frightening environment of a veterinarian's office began to put me off big-time. Never mind that that's where all of our previous animals had been put to sleep. Things change. And the day I carried Honeybear into our home, my world and how I perceive it had begun to change.

■ CHAPTER 4 ■

Intestinal Intransigence

Honeybear's slow, steady decline did nothing to dampen her enthusiasm for the activities that had defined her life. And I made certain she continued to be involved in everything we did.

When we went to the park to practice, HB was in her usual spot between the front seats. She'd sit in the van, snoozle the window and bark her head off as she watched the other dogs train. When it was her turn, she'd hop around joyously on stiff old legs, doing a few of the exercises she loved and could still accomplish.

On Friday evenings or Sunday mornings, when our training group got together for ring run-throughs, HB would burst out of the van to do scent articles, the signal exercise, and gleefully retrieve her dumbbell.

By spring of 2004, it was time for Cheddar to make his Novice debut. I brought him out on May 8 at the golden retriever specialty in San Juan Capistrano, where Honeybear had finished her long career a year earlier. Cheddar took second place to get his first Companion Dog leg. Which he followed the next day with a blue ribbon for his second leg.

Two for two. Great! We'd try to finish at the Kennel Club of Pasadena on May 22 and 23.

But on May 17 Honeybear vomited on the living room rug and immediately began having diarrhea. She vomited only once, but the diarrhea continued intermittently. We gave her Amforal. We gave her metronidazole. We tried both together. Barbara cooked boiled beef and rice, boiled chicken and rice. We slowed down the diarrhea, but we couldn't stop it.

Not that such intestinal intransigence was all that new with HB. About the time she had approached 12 years of age, she had begun having periodic bouts of loose bowels. Most were short-term. I'd give her a few Amforal tablets and the episode would subside. Later we settled into a routine where every few days, usually in the morning, she'd have diarrhea for one bowel movement. I'd ignore it, do nothing. Her next bowel movement would be normal and we'd go on from there. But this was different. There was a doggedness about it that we hadn't encountered before.

We had planned to drive to Pasadena on May 20, set up in Brookside Park on May 21 and compete in the trials on May 22 and 23. Two chances for Cheddar to get his third CD leg, his first title.

On the morning of May 19, I loaded the van. Then, at two o'clock that afternoon, I cancelled our hotel reservation and began unloading the van. It had become clear that HB shouldn't travel, and I sure didn't want to cope with diarrhea in a hotel room. (Board her? Don't even think about it!) So much for the Pasadena shows. Cheddar's third leg would have to wait.

I took Honeybear to Apollo Animal Hospital later that afternoon. Dr. Toben drew blood for a total body function analysis and took abdominal X-rays. None of which revealed anything conclusive. But he noted that she was beginning to get dehydrated, so he put her on IV fluids.

I picked her up at eight o'clock that evening when Dr. Toben made rounds. She would have to be on IV fluids for several days, but I didn't want to leave her there alone all night. No one would be on duty again until early the next morning. So for a couple of days I dropped her off at 7 A.M. and picked her up late in the afternoon.

Our decision not to go to Pasadena proved to be a wise one.

We had a summer training group on Friday evenings, the Dog Daze Gang. Nine of us had rented the baseball field at Buffalo Ridge Park. There, under better-than-daylight conditions, we'd set up a ring and run each other through the obedience exercises. The park was only 15 minutes from home. Sometimes Barbara would drive over and videotape our run-throughs — the "game films."

Having cancelled the Pasadena trip, I was free to train with the group on May 20. I took Cheddar and Bebop. Barbara came a bit later. Honeybear stayed home in the kitchen ... on the tile floor. Barbara remained at Dog Daze only long enough to tape Cheddar's Open and Utility runs, then she hustled home.

When I arrived home about 10:15, Barbara looked frazzled. "I just finished cleaning up the kitchen," she told me. "Honeybear really let fly while I was gone. There was diarrhea everywhere."

"Oh wow!" I said, "think what that would have been like in a carpeted hotel room in Southern California."

That big explosion in the kitchen was the last time HB ever lost control. Several days of IV fluids laced with antibiotics stemmed the crisis. Her bowel movements were still soft, but she no longer had diarrhea. We would struggle to maintain that delicate balance for the rest of her life.

It wasn't that she felt bad. Sure, she was closing in on her 15th birthday, but the sparkle remained in her eyes and heaven knows the want-to was still there.

Through it all, she was still pleasing her many fans in yet another way.

■ ■ ■

Remembering to Breathe: Inside Dog Obedience Competition was published early in 2004. As spring turned into summer, the word had gotten around. Several reviews in dog-related publications had said, in effect, "If you love dogs, you gotta read this!" A lively discussion was underway in Internet chat rooms. Sales were brisk.

All of which led to requests to autograph the book. We'd go out of town to compete in a trial. Inevitably someone would approach me, book in hand. First they'd want to know if Honeybear was with us. After they had petted her and told her what a great girl she was, they'd ask me to autograph the book. "If you'll let me take it home, *both* of us will autograph it," I'd reply. "Then I'll mail it right back." The offer was always accepted with delight.

And so it came to pass that well into her 15th year my old white-faced girl was autographing books — quite an operation to be sure. The enterprise took place on the grooming table in our utility room.

As our bath towels get old and begin to fray, they become the "dog towels." We'd spread one of the dog towels on top of the table and HB would stand on it. I'd place the book on the towel in front of and to the right of HB's right front paw, holding it open to the page facing the front cover. The ink pad would be positioned so that Barbara could lift HB's paw, place it firmly on the ink pad, then firmly onto the page.

That was the easy part. Getting the ink off HB's paw before she hit our off-white carpet was another matter. The ink refused to give up. I'd move the book and the ink pad out of the way. Barbara would slide into their place a basin of warm, soapy water. Then she'd dip HB's paw into the basin and scrub with a wash cloth. She'd test her success by placing HB's paw firmly on the towel. No dice! It still left a perfect black paw print. Scrub and test, scrub and test — the cycle often had to be repeated six or eight times before it was safe to let HB charge out of there to get her Bonz for an autographing session well done.

After Honeybear's first autographing session, whenever I'd say, "HB's got to autograph a book," Barbara would moan, "Oh God!" Quickly we learned to do five or six at a time.

As I write this, there are still several dog towels around here featuring multiple HB autographs.

■ ■ ■

Dr. Toben and I talked frequently. I'd tell him how, by the grace of Amforal and metronidazole and boiled chicken and rice, we were keeping the diarrhea at bay ... just barely. It had been weeks since HB had had a normal bowel movement. "Ploppy yellow poops," is how I'd describe it. But only when we took her outside, never in the house. Under the heavy medication, she was in control of her bowels, just not what they produced.

"How's she feeling otherwise?" Dr. Toben would ask. And I'd tell him what was happening every morning. I'd take Cheddar out in the backyard to do a little heeling, a figure eight, his daily scent articles. Honeybear would stand behind our huge plate glass windows and bark her head off until I'd relent, bring Cheddar inside and take her out there. We'd heel a couple of minutes and do a couple of scent articles. Then I'd open the door so HB could lead the charge to the kitchen where everyone would get a Bonz.

By early June it was obvious we had enough control that I could risk the trip to Flagstaff and give Cheddar a two-trial shot at finishing his CD.

■ ■ ■

Flagstaff Kennel Club has never-ending problems with the location of their annual all-breed dog show and obedience trial.

There is a perfect show venue in the heart of Flagstaff, Northern Arizona University. The campus even features a domed football stadium. Whether all or parts of the show would be held under the dome or on the campus lawns, the setting has much to offer.

Flagstaff Kennel Club has approached the university several times across the years, only to hit a brick wall. That impenetrable barrier is the university's refusal to allow recreational vehicles on campus. Any large dog show becomes, for one weekend, the recreational vehicle capital of the world. Which makes the RV ban the kiss of death.

As a result, the club has for years made do with marginally adequate facilities. For several years the show was held on the athletic fields of Coconino County High School. The lion's share of the parking was down the hill and far away from the rings, especially the obedience rings. They were always situated at the back of the show area — adjacent to a lovely stand of ponderosa pines, but a challenging schlep from the parking lot, made worse by the oxygen-poor air at 7,000 feet of altitude.

Several years ago the club bailed out of the high school facility and moved their show to the Coconino County Fairgrounds. Obedience competitors arrived to find their rings scrunched in between two buildings. Setups had to be around the corner of a building, making the rings impossible to see from those setups. The *piece de resistance,* however, was the trees and bushes that were growing *inside* the obedience rings.

In 2004 the club relocated the entire show/trial configuration to another part of the fairgrounds.

The club president was a lady I've gotten to know over the years. I talked with her on the telephone a couple of weeks before the June 5 and 6 trials. She was bubbling with enthusiasm. "We have a wonderful new location within the fairgrounds," she said. She went on to tell me that the entire show would be strung out along the straightaway of the racetrack, in front of the grandstand. "We're putting up a huge white tent," she told me. "The rings will be under that tent, in the shade."

Sounded good. So off we went on Friday morning to set up for the Saturday and Sunday shows.

Sure enough, there was the huge white tent stretched across the racetrack, right in front of the grandstand. And next to the tent were our three obedience rings lined up side-by-side in the late morning sun.

There is no doubt in my mind that the show chairman was telling the truth as she perceived it when we talked a couple of weeks before the shows. When those in charge of dog shows talk/think about the event, in their mind's eye they see the conformation rings, where the "beauty pageant" part of the show — the revenue-generating part — will be held.

Obedience is an afterthought. And that's just what obedience competitors have come to expect. We're the "other guys," and more often than not our ring accommodations are significantly inferior to the setup of the conformation rings.

One year in Lompoc, California, the obedience rings — rope stretched between rebar — were on a barren lot with a few parking spaces. Down the street, one block away, the conformation rings were festive with white posts and white chain. Tables at the ring entrances were adorned with flowers, and pots of flowers were strategically placed around the rings.

The conformation area was also where the port-a-johns were located — a city block removed from the obedience rings. I guess the show committee figured obedience competitors don't have to go. Or if they do, they can darn well hold it.

So why was I not surprised a couple of years later when I learned that Lompoc Kennel Club had dropped obedience from their late-summer show?

The sight that greeted us that Friday morning as we drove into the Flagstaff show grounds also came as no surprise. *Yep!* I thought. *Business as usual.*

Just outside the racetrack the ground was sandy with weeds but no grass. Not a good place to set up our tent, chairs, crates, etc. But opposite the first turn was a row of nine horse stalls. They were reasonably clean, covered and close to our rings. So we decided to forego our tent and set up in a stall. First, though, I'd walk the dogs.

I helped Honeybear out of the van, stood her on the ground and down she went. I helped her up but she crumpled again. "My God, Barbara," I said, "HB can't stand up anymore."

I put her back in the van and we walked Bebop, Cheddar and Noché. "Let's go ahead and set up," I said, "then we'll go back to the hotel. Before we check in, I'll try to walk Honeybear on the grass. If the same thing happens, we'll come back, get our stuff and make a beeline for home."

When we arrived at the Residence Inn, I pulled up beside a large patch of grass. HB hopped out of the van and nonchalantly went about her business. Then it dawned on me. Even though we had arrived at the show site before 11 o'clock that morning, the sandy ground outside the racetrack was hot. Noché, Bebop and Cheddar had managed on the hot surface, but Honeybear, unsteady at best, couldn't handle it.

None of that surprised me. For years I had commented on how much more intense the sun seemed at 7,000 feet. I had noticed that my head and face sunburned much more rapidly at that altitude. And 80 degrees in Flagstaff felt like 90 in Phoenix.

After lunch we went back to the show site; I wanted to play ball with Cheddar outside the rings, let him decide that was a fun place to be. Before we parked close to our setup, we walked the dogs in the woods outside the track area. HB was fine in the shade under the pines. But when I got her out of the van near the setup, she crumpled again. I had to carry her into the covered stall.

I threw the ball for Cheddar a few times on the track outside the ring. The dirt was packed and it seemed to be a good surface for obedience competition. Then we went back to the hotel.

Late that afternoon a friend called. Irate! She had driven over from Los Angeles and would be showing a toy poodle in Open B and Utility B the next two days. They had arrived at the show site after we had returned to the hotel. She had taken the little dog onto the track just outside the rings and the surface had burned his feet. Her tirade was my first clue as to the furor that would erupt the next morning.

We were lucky on Saturday morning. Novice B started at eight o'clock. Cheddar and I were tenth in the ring, and that allowed us to finish the individual exercises before the surface really heated up. Later, some of the intact male dogs refused to sit in the ring. A Visla did not sit once during his Novice run — not to start an exercise, not during the heeling pattern, not at front. "No way I'm going to put my balls down on that," he said.

Midway through the morning we heard an announcement over the PA system. Something like, "Flagstaff Kennel Club wants to apologize for the show conditions here this morning. We want to assure you that our show will not be held at this location next year."

Well! It would be one of the historic moments in dog obedience competition if a host club made a public apology prompted only by the fact that conditions in the obedience rings were God-awful. No, there was more to it than that. There were nine conformation rings under the "big top." The surface in each was several inches of loose dirt. As the show got underway and the handlers began running and kicking up that dirt, the inside of the tent became a cloud of dust.

One exhibitor recalled, "We were eating dirt, and white dogs turned brown."

Our Novice B class had 31 entries. By the time the individual exercises were finished, it was nearly noon. The sun was blazing and the floor of our ring was scorching hot. No way the long sits and downs could be held there. Our judge and the AKC obedience representative conferred interminably; it must have gone on for 20 minutes. Finally they asked the people in two E-ZUP tents near ringside if they would vacate temporarily. The folks obliged and the group exercises were done in successive groups of six, three dogs to a tent.

Later, when our judge had all the qualifiers and their dogs assembled — not in the ring but in the shade of the two E-ZUP tents — she said, "Before I hand out the ribbons, let me say that I hope each and every one of you will write a letter to Flagstaff Kennel Club protesting the deplorable conditions in the obedience rings here this morning."

Cheddar and I won the class with a 195.5. Only to learn that we had tied for high in trial with a miniature poodle out of the Open A class. A runoff would be necessary, but certainly not in the obedience rings.

Another conference between the judge and the AKC rep. By now it was just past noon. Several of the conformation rings had shut down for the lunch break. So the rep decided the runoff would be held in an empty conformation ring under the tent.

At the time, Cheddar was a month shy of his second birthday, immature and still highly distractable. Not exactly a seasoned obedience dog. When we entered the tent his eyes got big as saucers and his head seemed to be on a swivel: *Ooh! What's this?* We warmed up a little bit outside the ring, and Cheddar's attention was everywhere.

I've walked many a beach in the Caribbean, and the surface inside the ring reminded me of the footing just inshore of the tidemark, several inches of loose sand. Only this "beach" also featured an abundance of bait, dropped during the morning classes. So we had a cacophony of sounds reverberating off the tent to go with bad footing on a surface that offered a delightful cornucopia of tempting smells.

Neither team heeled well. We heeled worse. Oh well. Cheddar had won a large Novice B class and gone second high in trial under terrible conditions. Darn good for such a young dog.

Several times that morning when I wanted to give Honeybear a chance to pee, I carried her in my arms, maybe 30 yards, to a tiny patch of grass, set her down, then carried her back to her crate in the horse stall.

Putting it all together, the Flagstaff Kennel Club 2004 show weekend was a treacherous place for dogs. So when Cheddar finished his Companion Dog title on Saturday I said to Barbara, "We've got what we came for. Why cope with this situation again tomorrow? Let's go home."

Which we did.

■ CHAPTER 5 ■

Doing the Right Thing

Back home we settled into a relentless tug of war: Honeybear's determination to produce diarrhea versus every diarrhea-inhibiting medication in the pharmacopeia of veterinary medicine. The result? The "soft poops." A series of fecal smears and fecal-enteric panels revealed nothing of significance. Neither did a barium X-ray.

Through it all, HB stood at the window each morning and barked her way into the backyard, where she'd do scent articles (flawlessly) or the signal exercise. Or both.

Meanwhile, getting up off the floor became more and more difficult for her, and her rear end became more and more unstable. Dr. Toben and I had many conversations about her bowel problems, our inability to stop them and the likelihood that the root cause was cancer. Most of those conversations ended with me saying, "Nevertheless, I predict that when she goes it'll be because she can no longer get up off the floor."

Later that summer Dr. Toben offered me a more radical diagnostic option. A surgical procedure where they'd slice open HB's abdomen along the midline and take little sections of her intestines to be examined for cancer.

There was no way I'd put her through that, but we did discuss it thoroughly. "OK," I said, "suppose you find something. Then what?"

He paused only briefly. "There have been situations," he said, "where what I've found was so advanced that I've gotten on the phone with the client while the animal was still on the operating table. I've told them, 'I don't think we should let Fluffy wake up from the anesthetic.'"

"I'm not going to subject Honeybear to major exploratory surgery at this point," I told him.

I can't remember a time, across the nearly two decades of our relationship, when Chuck Toben and I weren't on the same page. And it was clear that we were this time. He didn't really want to slice HB open at that point; he was giving me full disclosure of my options. "I'm offering this to you because most of my clients need answers," he said.

"Well I don't need answers," I replied emphatically. "I need to protect my dog." And that was the end of that.

Across nearly 15 years, what HB wanted most out of life was to be with me. And that never changed. It must have been terribly hard for her to constantly get up and follow me around the house — even though she was getting prednisone and Etogesic on alternate days. But I'd walk through the house, and if I chanced to glance back, that old white face would be a few feet behind me, looking up at my back. "It must drive her crazy," I told Barbara. "I get up to go to another room for only a second, then I go right back to where we started."

■ ■ ■

As Cheddar had trained for Novice, we had also worked on the Open and Utility exercises. As a result, when he finished his CD he was close to being ready to enter Open competition.

Prescott Arizona Kennel Club scheduled an AKC-sanctioned match for August 15 at the Chino Valley Community Center. It would be a good dress rehearsal for the Prescott shows coming up in the middle of September at the same site. It would be a simple trip; drive up in the morning, do our thing, return in the afternoon.

So we signed up and kept our fingers crossed that HB would be able to travel. Of course she wasn't entered, but where we went Honeybear went, or we didn't go.

August 15 came. All systems were go, so we all piled into the van. Although we were able to park right outside the fence at the show site, we chose not to work out of the van. Setting up our tent and putting the dogs in their soft crates was all part of acclimating Cheddar to the dog show environment. Scarcely two years old, he was still green, green, green.

At the match, Cheddar chose to bring the dumbbell around the high jump. Aside from that little blunder, his Open run was quite good. It was obvious he'd be back in mid-September to make his Open debut.

Dorothy Holmes was also there, working her Rottweilers out of her van. They were parked behind our tent, outside the fence. Dorothy was an old-timer around the obedience rings. She had known us for almost as long as we had been showing in obedience. She loved Honeybear, and she knew my sweet old girl was losing ground.

After Cheddar was finished in the ring, and in preparation for going home, I started to get Honeybear out of her crate and take her for a walk. Dorothy was close by. "Just a minute," she said. "I just want to pet Honeybear and tell her goodbye … just in case I don't see her again." With that she stepped forward, hugged HB, told her what a great girl she was, and said goodbye. One of the sweetest gestures I've ever known. And devastating!

I had HB on leash at the time, so I said, rather abruptly I'm afraid, "Let's go be a good girl." Then we moved quickly out into the large, open field, as far away as we could get. It was either that or burst into tears right there in front of our tent.

Two weeks later Chino Valley Canine Club was holding a fun match at Memory Park in Chino Valley. That one would be a *must*. Unlike sanctioned matches, fun matches permit training in the ring, definitely what Cheddar needed at that stage of his fledgling career. And I had entered HB in Utility at that match, just so I could let her go into the ring and frisk through the scent articles. She'd love it.

For many months, Honeybear had been panting heavily, except when she was stretched out, relaxing or asleep. In the middle of the night she'd raise her head and begin to pant. We always knew when she was awake; we were, too.

On Wednesday afternoon, August 25, I was in my office, working at my desk. I heard HB panting, coming down the hall toward the room where I was working. I was engrossed in what I was doing, but I was aware that she was coming … and coming … and coming. Almost subconsciously I wondered what was taking her so long; it's a distance of only 20 feet.

As she came through the door, I realized what the problem was. Her rear end and hind legs were dragging behind her as she pulled herself forward with her front legs. I quickly helped her to her feet, and for the rest of the day she got around just fine on four legs. But the handwriting was on the wall.

After that incident, I decided the trip to Chino Valley would be too much for HB. So I planned to leave her at home with Barbara and take only Cheddar and Bebop.

Except that Sunday morning found the battery in my van dead as a doornail. Enough already! We stayed home.

Monday morning, as usual, Honeybear stood at the window and barked her head off as I worked Cheddar in the backyard. Then she joyously emerged from the house to do a perfect set of scent articles. After which everybody raced to the kitchen and got a Bonz.

At two o'clock Tuesday morning we awoke to a loud, persistent banging. Barbara and I shot out of bed. I turned on the light. Honeybear was on the tile floor in the doorway to the master bathroom. She was flailing wildly, banging the door against the wall, panic in her eyes as she struggled to get up off the floor.

I helped her up, but she sank back down. Again and again I helped her up only to watch her collapse. Her rear end simply wouldn't hold her.

"That's it," I said as I headed for my office. At 2:15 I dialed Apollo Animal Hospital, leaving a message I knew would be picked up first thing in the morning. I was sobbing so hard I could hardly speak. I said something like, "The time has come. We need to put Honeybear to sleep. I want it done *here* as soon as possible in the morning."

I knew how devastating that news would be when the Apollo staff arrived shortly after dawn. We were like family there, and they adored Honeybear.

I went back to the bedroom and got HB situated near the bed, on the carpet. She was exhausted. Soon her panting stopped and I knew she was asleep.

It was Tuesday, August 31, and unfortunately Tuesday mornings are surgery mornings at Apollo. When the office manager called back shortly after sunrise, the message she left was that Dr. Toben would be in surgery all morning, but he had said to tell me he'd be at our house at noon.

Honeybear wouldn't eat her breakfast. In fact, she had scarcely touched her food for the last 24 hours. HB had been the most food-driven dog I had ever known. For a long time I had been telling people, "The day Honeybear stops eating I'll know the end has come." And here we were.

Almost on the stroke of 12 noon a black Toyota Avalon pulled up in front of the house, and I knew the moment I had dreaded for the past several years had come.

Up the front walk he came. The same Charles G. Toben who had first held Honeybear in his hands on a Saturday morning in February 1990. Scarcely two hours after I had picked her up from the breeder. She was seven weeks old, a tiny bundle of fluff. In fact, "Fluff Puff" was what the breeder's daughter had called her.

Dr. Toben had pronounced her fit (and cute) that morning, and the most fulfilling adventure of my life had begun. Across nearly 15 years, Chuck Toben — first HB's vet, but ultimately a warm, close friend — had presided over Honeybear's well-being. Now he was coming to preside over the last breaths she'd ever take.

Some sage has pointed out that one of the advantages of growing old is that you get to see how people's stories turn out. Trouble is, with animals you don't need to grow old. As they used to say in the Nationwide Insurance commercials, "Life comes at you fast."

Honeybear hadn't moved around much that morning. I had managed to get her outside a couple of times. But by late morning she had settled down on the tile walkway that surrounds our sunken living room. It wasn't that she was in pain, she just couldn't anymore.

This was the dog who had loved to play ball, who would tear across the polo field and grab the ball in a skidding cloud of dust. Who had retrieved and jumped and heeled smartly at my side all the way to an Obedience Trial Championship.

Now, though, it was clear my big girl had given up. Her old eyes no longer sparkled. And the spot on the tile walkway was where Dr. Toben and veterinary technician Omar Paredes found her when they came through the front door.

Dr. Toben took one look at HB and said, "You're doing the right thing, Willard." Then they went to work. Omar was carrying a black bag. He reached into that bag and handed Dr. Toben a small portable clipper. Dr. Toben shaved an area of Honeybear's left front leg. Then he slipped a needle into the cephalic vein. The syringe was loaded with 12 ml. of sodium pentothal, a lethal dose.

I sat on the floor next to Honeybear and stroked her head. Barbara sat in a large chair behind me, crying softly. As the sodium pentothal began to flow into her vein, Dr. Toben said, "Talk to her, Willard."

I had known for a long time what my final words to my big girl would be. They would be the same words I had said to her each morning as I brushed her. So they came easily. "We did it, Honeybear. We did it together."

After about 30 seconds I knew her breathing had stopped. Dr. Toben checked her heart with his stethoscope. "She's gone, Willard," he said.

They had brought with them a large green bag. Now they lifted the body of the dog who had changed my life, slipped it into the bag and tied it shut. Dr. Toben knew I would be having Honeybear cremated. He offered to take her body with him and have it delivered to Pet and Animal Lovers Service (PALS), an animal crematory I had chosen. "No," I said, "we've been together through a lot. She'll stay with me now."

Earlier that morning I had called PALS to see if they could cremate HB that day. Yes, they could handle it at four o'clock that afternoon. No way I was going to turn my big girl over to anyone in the interim.

Dr. Toben understood. He has always understood. So they packed up their stuff and prepared to leave. The last thing Dr. Toben said to me before they went out the door was, "You did the right thing, Willard."

Yes, I had. When my big girl needed me to be strong, I had been. And I was at peace with my decision.

I watched Toben and Paredes go down the front walk and get into the car. Then I closed the door, pounded on it with my fist and sobbed, "I didn't want it to ever end."

Then I turned around. At the end of the most wonderful adventure of my life there was only that big green bag on the living room floor.

■ CHAPTER 6 ■

Ashes to Ashes

Honeybear had her own special spot in the van. For how many tens of thousands of miles had she snuggled in the well between the front seats? Occasionally I'd reach down and stroke her head. Or she'd put her chin against my leg and look up at me — particularly as the afternoon wore on and it was time to begin to work me for her supper.

It was only proper that her final ride in the van be made in her special spot. So at about 3:30 that afternoon I lifted the green bag off the floor. For one reason or another I had lifted Honeybear thousands of times, but she had never been so heavy. I understood what they mean by "dead weight." Barbara and I managed to get her into the van and between the seats. Then off we went.

PALS is located in an industrial neighborhood on the west side of Phoenix. I had been there before — ostensibly to do research for a column I wrote in *Borderlines*, the magazine of the Border Collie Society of America. My visit had resulted in a two-part series: "Death and Dying and Dogs."

All of which emanated from a slightly ulterior motive. As Honeybear aged, I was not oblivious to where we were heading, and I wanted to be prepared. I knew that the day of HB's death would be no time to scramble, physically and mentally, through a landscape of emotional hurt, trying to put together the whens, wheres and hows.

I knew the whats. When I die, I want to be cremated (and all the arrangements have been made and paid for). As my animals die, I'll have them cremated. Then I want their cremains mixed with mine and scattered in a favorite training spot.

But I need a lot of reassurance about the cremation of my best friends. The big hang-up has nothing to do with their being burned up (or my being burned up). "Ashes to ashes, dust to dust." I'm OK with that. What I'm *not* OK with is even the remotest possibility that the cremains returned to me might be those of some animal other than mine.

About the time HB passed her 12th birthday I could no longer ignore the handwriting that glared off the wall. Finding out how to make the endgame as fail-safe as possible became imperative.

A long time ago I learned that the best way to find out all I wanted to know about anything I wanted to know was to don the mantle of writer and zero in. Across nearly half a century of writing, I've produced many an article, many a column motivated by my own need to know. So I got busy and researched the two-part series that eventually ran in *Borderlines*.

I quickly learned that many who choose cremation know nothing about it. Which makes them vulnerable. That was me! But it didn't take much networking before the chaff began to fall away from the wheat.

Dr. Toben spoke well of a small company called Pet and Animal Lovers Services. As did a couple of other people whose opinions I respect. So I made an appointment and visited with Katherine Heuerman, the owner. Her story of how she came to start the business was an eye-opener.

In 1986, recently divorced, Katherine moved from Nebraska to Phoenix to start a new life. She brought along an aging

Irish setter named Duffy, and Sarah, a Sheltie. Shortly before Christmas that year, 15-year-old Duffy was diagnosed with inoperable cancer and had to be put to sleep. Katherine decided to have her old friend cremated — separately so that Duffy's cremains could be returned to her.

She assumed she'd get them back within a few days. A week went by, then a second, no cremains. Katherine called the crematory and was told, "Oh, we've been so busy." Finally, after three weeks, Duffy's cremains were returned. By that time, Katherine was beside herself and angry. She called the crematory, pressed to speak to the owner and began asking aggressive questions.

Why had it taken so long? The owner was evasive, but the gist of it was they hadn't had time to get to her dog; they were *so* backed up. The more questions Katherine asked, the more she smelled a rat. She asked if she could tour the facility. "It isn't our policy to allow inspections," the owner replied. That ended the conversation.

Deeply troubled, Katherine stewed over the incident for two weeks. Then, late one afternoon, she drove to the crematory. There she encountered a locked gate and a high wall surrounding the property. She found a crate, stood on it and looked over the wall. The yard was filthy and littered with bags containing dead animals — people's pets! The stench made her queasy.

So *this* was how Duffy had been treated while Katherine endured the interminable wait. And the scene raised nagging doubts in her mind. Had the cremains that had finally been returned to her really been Duffy's? She'd never know.

As it turned out, the appalling incident had a silver lining. Katherine had been thinking of starting a business in Phoenix. That evening, as she viewed the ugly scene on the other side of the wall, it all came together in her mind. She'd do what she could to keep the experience she'd gone through with Duffy from happening to others. In less than six months, PALS was launched with the mission of offering to others who were parting with their best friends the service, comfort and support she had been denied.

During our visit, Katherine gave me a small book (now out of print), *The Final Farewell: Preparing for and Mourning the Loss of Your Pet*. Katherine had written the book with Marty Tousley, R.N. In it I found nine questions that should help the neophyte understand the cremation option and avoid a disappointing, upsetting experience.

1. Is the crematory a reputable one, well established with a solid reputation in the community?
2. What services are available, and what are the costs? Descriptions, fees and contracts should be in writing.
3. Are preplanning and payment plans available?
4. Does the crematory offer separate cremation, and how is that defined?
5. Does the crematory permit you to be present during the cremation of your pet?
6. Can you tour the facility?
7. Will a crematory representative pick up and transport your pet's remains?
8. Will the crematory prepare your pet's body for viewing or for a memorial service?
9. How will your pet's cremains be returned to you, and in what time frame?

Long before I had reached decision time with Honeybear, I had decided PALS would be best for us. So as we took HB for her final ride, I was comfortable with what we were about to do.

■ ■ ■

PALS is a low, slump block building — two buildings, actually, one behind the other — sandwiched into a warehousing/light industrial neighborhood. It sits across the street from a cement block company, acres and acres of cement blocks.

I pulled up in front and got out. Barbara waited in the van with HB while I went inside. Jamie, whom I had talked to on the phone twice that morning, greeted me. Yes, they were expecting us, and if I'd pull the van around back, they'd help us unload Honeybear and the process would begin.

In the back, at the end of a long, narrow driveway, two men were waiting with a cart. "I'll help you," one of the men said, and he headed toward the back of the van with the cart. I guess most people arrive with the bodies of their dead animals in the back of their vehicles. By the time the man had recovered and brought the cart around to the front door, Barbara and I had struggled with that dead weight again and had gotten HB out of the well between the seats and onto Barbara's seat. I didn't explain. How could I expect anyone to appreciate why it was mandatory that Honeybear's last ride be taken in the spot that had been hers and hers alone for countless tens of thousands of miles?

Before wheeling HB into the rear building, the attendant explained that there was a special, private viewing area where the family could say their final goodbyes. Did we want to use that area? No, I told him, we had said our goodbyes at home. Indeed, I had been saying goodbye to my big girl for a long, long time. I wondered how many dozens of times in the past year I had shed a tear or two as I brushed Honeybear early in the morning, all the while saying, "We did it, Honeybear! We did it together!"

While the cart with the big green bag on top disappeared into the rear building, I backed the van down the long, narrow driveway to park it in the tiny front lot.

As we got out, Barbara picked up a small bag that she had been holding on her lap since we left home. It was a decorative gift bag with a golden retriever on the side. Inside were three items I had chosen to send along with Honeybear: a tennis ball, a copy of *Remembering to Breathe* and a small card. That card had accompanied the stuffed toy dog who represented the golden retriever puppy I was getting for that long-ago Christmas of 1989. The card said:

> *I, Skip, promise to*
> *love and hug you*
> *forever and ever*
> *because you were*
> *given to me*
> *by*
> *Barbara*

I had tacked that card up on the bulletin board behind my desk. Across the years, I had looked at it often — particularly at times in Honeybear's life when things seemed grim. Now, at the end, as I removed the card from my bulletin board, I took comfort in knowing that there had not been a single day in HB's life — not one! — when I hadn't done my very best with her and for her. And it seemed imperative that my pledge accompany her into eternity.

So with the little decorative bag in hand we went inside. The front building houses offices, a reception area and a private lounge for grieving families. Our destination was the building in the rear where cremations are done.

As we started down the long hall leading to the rear, we came to several shelves displaying many attractive urns. Barbara stopped to look at them, but I had little interest. My intention was to retrieve HB's cremains in the white plastic container that was offered as standard with the cremation service. After all, the container would be only temporary until Honeybear's ashes were scattered with mine in a park where, alone, we had spent thousands of afternoons that cannot adequately be described. So we paused only briefly, then continued down the hall toward the cremation building.

We hadn't gone far when someone came hurrying up behind us. It was Marcella, another person I had seen in the front office. "I saw that bag you're carrying," she told Barbara, "and I want you to have this." She handed Barbara a small pin, a tiny dog with wings and a halo.

Marcella could scarcely have guessed how much that gesture meant to me. My office is a gallery reflecting Honeybear's accomplishments across an obedience career that spanned more than a dozen years. Every inch of every wall is covered with ribbons, trophies and photos. Including that last ribbon she ever received on that memorable morning in San Juan Capistrano when, at 13½, she won everything in sight. I have affixed Marcella's pin to that ribbon, like a tie tack. It represents how I'd like to think Honeybear is today.

Albert met us as we entered the rear building. "It'll be just a few minutes," he told us, "while I prepare Honeybear for cremation." We waited in a small anteroom — they call it the "witness room" — just outside the cremation area. The furnishings were spartan: two metal folding chairs, a small desk with a phone, a small refrigerator. "Help yourselves," Albert said, gesturing toward the refrigerator, "there's bottled water and soft drinks in there." Then he left the room.

I looked around. A large window offered an unobstructed view of the cremation machines. Some call them ovens. The correct name is *retorts*. I knew from my earlier research that the one to my right was used for multiple cremations. The one on the left was for individual cremations. That was where Honeybear would be reduced to ashes.

Behind me was a row of shelves, labeled "Monday, Tuesday ..." etc. Each shelf was stacked with white, hard plastic boxes, and each box was labeled with a client's name. The boxes contained cremains waiting to be delivered to veterinarians' offices on scheduled days. Mine would not be delivered, and I thought, *That's how I'll carry HB out of here today.*

I had requested a witnessed cremation — that is, we'd be present for the whole process. That was important to me for two reasons.

First, although PALS had an excellent reputation, screwups can happen, and I wanted to make darn sure the cremains that would sit atop the bookcase in my office for the rest of my life would be Honeybear and only Honeybear.

Second, Honeybear and I had been *so* close, joined at the soul. And I felt a gut-level imperative to stay with her now. In the most wonderful adventure of my life, Honeybear had gone the distance with me. Now I would stay the course with her. Nothing in Honeybear's life had been as important to her as the nearness of me. I would not deny her that here at the end.

So we sat in the folding chairs, drank a Pepsi and watched through the window. Before long, Albert wheeled another cart into the cremation room. There was Honeybear, my big girl who had run and jumped and retrieved and heeled and frisked and tail-wagged through the most fulfilling chapter in my life. Who less than 36 hours ago had done her final obedience exercise, two perfect scent articles. And now she was stiff and motionless.

Albert positioned the cart just in front of the retort on the left. Then he walked over to our tiny witness room, opened the door and said, "We're ready. You can come in."

"I'll stay here and watch through the window," Barbara said. I picked up the little bag with the happy-looking golden retriever on the side and followed Albert. The cremation room was hot and the decibel level was deafening. Everything about cremation is hot and noisy.

Albert stood back while I approached the cart. HB was on her side, so I snuggled the three items against her tummy — the tennis ball, the book that told the story of our once-in-a-lifetime adventure, and the little card with my pledge on it. I said nothing. I didn't need to. Then I stepped back.

"Would you like to remove her collar?" Albert asked.

"No," I said, "that's her ring collar." No way he could understand the journey that collar had taken, what that journey had meant.

Albert walked over to the retort, pressed a button and the door opened, revealing a blast furnace; no other way to describe it.

"See," he said, "there's nothing in there." Then he took a long-handled rake and drew it toward us along the bottom of the chamber. It collected nothing. The chamber was devoid of any residue from earlier cremations.

Finally he wheeled the cart close to the open door. "You're going to see flames flare up right away," he said, "because her coat will ignite instantly." I nodded.

The top of the cart was level with the floor of the cremation chamber. Using the rake, Albert easily slid HB off the cart and into the 1,635-degree chamber. The last time I ever saw my big girl, she was bursting into flames.

Then Albert pushed the button again and the door closed. "It'll be about 45 minutes," he said. So I went back into the witness room to wait.

A short time later Barbara said, "Do you mind if I walk back up front? I'd like to look around." I didn't mind. She had been gone only a few minutes when she returned carrying a green, tan and brown mottled urn. "Isn't this pretty?" she asked.

"Well, yes," I replied. Indeed it was. "But I was going to just keep her in the plastic container they'll give us. This is only temporary until her ashes are scattered with mine."

She looked at me for a moment, then she said, softly, "She deserves better than that."

Yes, Barbara was right. It was about respect for a life that had mattered so much. "OK," I said, "let's get it."

The wait continued. Several times Albert opened the door of the retort and looked in. Then he moved the contents around with his long-handled rake.

After nearly three-quarters of an hour had passed, he opened the chamber door again and raked the cremains forward to the front of the chamber. They fell into a chute which emptied into a bucket he had placed at the bottom of the chute. Then he brought the bucket to a work area just outside the room where we were waiting. There the cremains were allowed to cool.

The end product of cremation is bone fragments. When they had cooled sufficiently, Albert poured them into a processing machine to be pulverized into the smooth, powdery "ashes" we associate with cremation. That final step is cosmetic, to fulfill our concept of "ashes to ashes."

Finally Albert poured Honeybear's cremains into a plastic bag, tied it shut and placed it in the urn Barbara had picked out. "I put the cremains in a bag because sometimes an urn gets broken or the lid comes off," he told me. "This way, if there's an accident, the cremains won't spill all over the place."

Next he coated the rim of the urn with an adhesive substance and put the lid on. He secured the lid with two pieces of Scotch tape. "I don't like to seal these so tightly that later you have to break the urn if you want to open it," he told me. "But if you leave the tape on for 24 hours, the adhesive will hold."

That urn now sits atop a bookcase in my office. Between Honeybear's scent articles and a stuffed rooster, a toy she won on that morning when she concluded her career in grand style in San Juan Capistrano. Frankly, it's a poor substitute for the dog who so enriched my life for nearly 15 years. But it's all that's left that actually *is* Honeybear.

When we were finished at PALS, it was nearly 5:30. Albert walked us down that long driveway, all the way to our van. Then we drove home with HB in an urn on Barbara's lap. The space between the front seats was so empty ... and still is.

And August 31, 2004, became the first in a string of some 5,500 nights when I was not able to reach down and stroke Honeybear's soft head at my bedside.

CHAPTER 7

When Great Dogs Get to Heaven

"Hi Honeybear," God said. "I'm God."

"Hi God," Honeybear replied. "How did you know my name? There are trillions of animals on Earth, and … "

God interrupted. "Oh, I've been a fan of yours for a long time," he said. "Remember that morning in Las Cruces, New Mexico, the day you finished your OTCH?"

"Oh yes!" Honeybear said, and her eyes sparkled. "Skippy was so happy that morning."

"Well," God continued, "I was there that morning. Remember, you had been having trouble jumping. You had refused the jump several times in practice. And that morning, when it came time for the directed jumping exercise, Skippy was almost praying out loud in the ring."

"Yeah," Honeybear said, "he was a basket case."

God chuckled. "Let's just say I gave you a little boost that morning."

Honeybear started to say thanks, but God waved her off. "No need for thanks," he said, "all of us up here are members of the Honeybear Fan Club."

Then God patted his left leg and said, "Now come with me, I want to show you something."

They hadn't gone very far when they came upon a large rectangular field of perfectly maintained green grass. At one end several Aleppo pine trees cast their shade over a bed of soft pine needles. The field was surrounded by a chain-link fence, punctuated here and there by gates.

For a moment, Honeybear stood stock still, staring in disbelief. Then she said, "Why it's the polo field, the very place where Skippy and I trained for thousands of afternoons, the place where I learned to be an OTCH dog."

God smiled. "Yes, Honeybear, it's the polo field from Paradise Valley Park, your favorite place on Earth. When they bulldozed it to construct that freeway interchange, I brought it up here. Just like great dogs, great training grounds go to Heaven."

God paused long enough to survey the dozen or so obedience rings set up on the polo field. Then he said, "Welcome to our Heavenly Training Facility. The greatest dogs and handlers in the history of competition obedience meet here to train and compete. And the temperature is always 65 degrees."

"Well, that beats Arizona summers," Honeybear said. But then her tail dropped. "I'm afraid I can't do much in the ring anymore," she told God. "I haven't jumped since the morning I finished my OTCH; my hips are shot. In fact, right before I left Earth I couldn't even get up off the floor."

God smiled again. "Come over here," he said. And he led her into a ring set up for Utility. "Give this jump a try," he told her, and he pointed to the bar jump.

Honeybear gulped. "That's set at 28 inches," she protested. "That was my jump height early in my career, before the AKC lowered the height requirements. And like I told you, I haven't been able to jump *anything* for five years."

"Go ahead," God said, "trust me. Besides, if you hit the bar, it'll just fall off."

God didn't give Honeybear time to think about that. "Ready?" he asked. And before she could reply, he cried, "BAR!"

Honeybear hesitated a second, then instinctively charged toward the jump and sailed over it.

God clapped his hands. "Way to go, Honeybear!" he yelled. "You cleared that bar by six inches."

Imagine that! Honeybear thought, *here's God, clapping for ME.* Then she trotted back to his side.

"You see, Honeybear," God said, "there is no hip dysplasia in Heaven."

Honeybear studied God's rugged face for a moment. Then she ventured, "How about deafness and cloudy vision?"

"Nah!" God said. "No deafness, no cataracts, not even cancer. Here in Heaven everybody feels great all the time."

"Wow!" Honeybear said, "does Skippy know about all this?"

God thought for just a moment. "I'm sure he does," he replied. "He believes that as one enters Heaven they are made whole again. He also believes that by and by the two of you will be back in the ring and you'll be at his side again. And because he believes so strongly, that will come to pass."

Honeybear wagged her tail furiously.

"When Skippy gets here," God continued, "the two of you can start to work on your HOTCH, your Heavenly OTCH."

"Is that like the OTCH we got back on Earth?" Honeybear asked.

"Well, the competition is really tough," God said, "because all the great dogs are here. But it's the same exercises, and we're bound by the AKC regulations. The most important difference is you need a million points to finish."

"A million points?!" Honeybear looked at God in disbelief.

"That's right," God said, "but remember, you have eternity to finish it."

So Honeybear curled up in the sunshine, on the polo field grass at ringside, to wait for Skippy.

■ CHAPTER 8 ■

Honeybear's Legacy

On the evening of Honeybear's death and cremation, I received an email of condolences from a friend. It began, "An era is over."

I quickly wrote back. Something like, "No, this is not the end of an era. Honeybear's legacy is so rich, so powerful that the Honeybear Era will last a long time."

Simply stated, nearly all the positive chapters in my life have stemmed directly from the influence of four females: my mother, Barbara, Debby Boehm ... and Honeybear.

On the day we lost HB my world was so different from my world on the day I carried her into our home as to be unrecognizable. For all the wonderful things Honeybear did for me and meant to me, her most potent contribution was that she changed my life, and indeed Barbara's life, forever.

Now, most mornings find me in some park at sunrise, training my dogs for competition obedience. And many weekends find us at practice matches or obedience trials — with a tent, a mat, chairs, crates, coolers, practice jumps, and assorted paraphernalia too diverse to mention. Oh, and a large cart on which to haul it from the parking lot to the setup area.

We arrive in a big van with an auxiliary generator and air conditioner. Before HB, I drove a car.

One morning each week, at dawn, Barbara and her little poodle Noché arrive many miles from home for an agility lesson. And one evening each week finds them in class at Jumping Chollas Agility Club.

With Barbara on the other end of the leash, Bebop became the first border collie breed champion in Arizona. But for Honeybear, there would have been no Bebop.

Fully a third of Barbara's real estate transactions emanate from contacts made in the world of dog sports. When she has a listing client with a dog or dogs who might be an impediment to showing the house, she says, "Not to worry!" She arranges for agents or prospective buyers to call her before showing. She arrives before the lookers and has the canine situation under control while they move about the house.

That's the same Barbara who was buffaloed by a rowdy, increasingly large puppy named Honeybear.

Had there been no Honeybear, hence no Bebop, we wouldn't be involved in Arizona Border Collie Rescue. I wouldn't have pulled a wonderful young border collie named Pete out of a shelter in St. George, Utah, one Thanksgiving Eve, thereby commuting his death sentence just hours before he was due to feel the needle.

Nor would I have brought another little BC rescue, Spot, into our home terrified, then two months later sent her strutting into her forever home.

Nor, as I write this, would I have recently adopted a little rescue border collie. He's bursting with want-to, and I call him Bravo! I've registered him as Lock-Eye Phantom of the Opera, and he'll be heard from in the world of competition obedience.

I would never have begun writing dog sports-oriented columns for *Front & Finish* and *Borderlines*. And the adventure that led to *Remembering to Breathe* would never have taken place.

That book has become a huge and unexpected part of the legacy of HB.

As I sat alone at this desk for two years writing *Remembering to Breathe,* what did I hope would be the outcome? For starters, that my efforts would actually result in a book. But I wasn't sure. For the preceding several years I had told myself, *This has been the greatest adventure of my life, it's a story screaming to be told.* Which is all fine and dandy in the abstract, but when it came time to commit ink to paper would there be a whole book there? And if there was, would anybody care?

Two sets of "who cares?" dynamics were converging on my project.

First, when I stepped back, got real in the most brutally honest way, I understood that the victories that HB and I shared, the defeats, the moments of glory, the pratfalls, were experiences in our own little world. Others congratulated us or expressed polite condolences, but our visceral reactions were just that, internal. Could I put those experiences on paper in such a way as to make them matter to readers? Only time would tell.

Second, you can sit in the privacy of a workroom and write day in and day out until you get a cerebral hernia, and the world doesn't care. You can grind out 350 pages of "Ask Me About My Grandkids." You aren't bothering the world, and the world isn't going to bother you.

The moment of truth doesn't come until your peerless prose interfaces with the real world. Until it's time for publishers to publish, reviewers to review, prospective readers to vote with their credit cards.

Once I knew I had a book — defined only by the weight of the manuscript — modest hopes began to form. Hopes that kindred souls in the dog obedience world would identify with the journey HB and I had taken and might enjoy reading about it. That it would sell a respectable number of copies (it has.) And that parts of it would hit their target, certain miscreants in the dog obedience world who had remained unexposed for far too long.

Eventually, at the beginning of 2004, *Remembering to Breathe* came out. And to my eternal delight all the right people loved it and all the right people hated me for it. I had told it like it was about Phoenix Field and Obedience Club (PFOC), a local organization that has for decades survived in moribund mediocrity for no other reason than because it's the only game in town.

By and by I learned that various PFOC and Coven members (many are one and the same) had indignantly vowed to boycott my book. Later, several of them approached my friends on the q.t., saying, "We vowed to boycott Willard's book, but I want to read it. Could I borrow yours?"

The answer, my friends assured me, was a resounding, "Are you kidding me?"

■ ■ ■

The ink was hardly dry on *Remembering to Breathe* when the feedback began pouring in.

Not surprisingly, the book seemed to resonate most with Novice A handlers. One of them, Madeleine from Georgia, wrote a review on the Amazon.com website. She said, "I stayed up 'til 2 A.M. I just couldn't wait to find out if HB and Skippy achieved their OTCH. This book is a real roller coaster, I actually cried at the end. It's as much a love story of a man and his dog as it is a fascinating look into the world of dog training and the obedience ring … If, like me, you are entering the world of competitive dog obedience, this book isn't only a good obedience primer (I got some great tips), it will make you much more confident going into the ring."

A Novice A trainer from Southern California wrote: "I have a feeling you'll never know the extent of 'treasured things' that have emanated from the publication of your book; you've given us all a gift."

She continued, "Last week I got up an hour early to finish reading (and crying over) *Remembering to Breathe*. I want to thank you for writing it. You wrote (and trained) from the heart, and your observations and experiences helped me to refocus my training. It's obvious that Honeybear was the only one you were trying to impress and that you *respected* her ... something I see missing in many teams. Thank you again for putting your journey into beautifully written and honest words."

Closer to home, Susan in Phoenix sent this touching message: "I am savoring every page in your book. I have to say I have cried about every fourth page and am incredulous that I have shared the same experiences/feelings as you in starting up in obedience. I have asked my husband to read your book as a birthday present to me. (I now have the words — your words — to express what it means to me to have a dog and seriously train one.)"

From Linda, a highly successful competition obedience and agility trainer and obedience judge. "I almost missed taking a shower before leaving for our club's annual awards banquet because I had to finish (your) book. Competing with a dog certainly has its ups and downs, and I think you captured the essence for many."

The local media chose to ignore *Remembering to Breathe*. Not a nibble. Nationally, though, the kudos were abundant. For instance:

The Midwest Book Review called *Remembering to Breathe* "An intriguing insider's story, spirited and revealing."

Rue Chagoll, writing for *Golden Retriever News*, concluded his piece this way: "You needn't ever have set foot near obedience competition, nor even own a golden retriever to appreciate and enjoy this story. If you've ever partnered with a dog to do anything — from therapy to agility, from flyball to field — you'll see a bit of yourself and your dog in Willard and Honeybear. This is neither a how-to book nor a bragging chronicle of accomplishment. *Remembering to Breathe* is more than anything a love story ... one you surely don't want to miss."

On the *Dogwise.com* website, a reviewer who used the nom de plume "goldenangel" gushed: "I couldn't put it down. Bought it on Saturday and finished it on Tuesday ... I thought no one could love and have bonded with their dog as much as me, but Willard takes it to another level. I cried along with their achievements and setbacks."

The most interesting review on Amazon.com was written by Karen, from Eau Claire, Wisconsin. She referred to herself as "an apprentice dog trainer." Buried in her review was an admission that she and her 14-month-old golden retriever, Katie, had experienced rough going earlier in their Novice A career — largely, I learned later, as a result of harsh and dispiriting training at the hands of an instructor who used the old jerk-em-around techniques. Karen was so discouraged that she was on the verge of "hanging it all up until I found and read this book."

I wanted to know more and to thank her for the accolades in her review. Some aggressive sleuthing allowed me to contact her and find out the rest of the story.

Yes, she told me, the early training using "the old method" had broken Katie's spirit. I learned that in the wake of reading *Remembering to Breathe* Karen had found a new instructor and a new training group in Minneapolis and was now traveling several hundred miles each week — after work! — to get instruction. And Katie was happy again. They had done well in a match and were planning to come out in Novice A late in 2006. Karen closed a recent letter with: "You and your book really made all the difference for me in helping restore my lost confidence resulting from those unfortunate training sessions with the force trainer."

■ ■ ■

The book's impact began to hit me up close and in person the spring after it came out. At every dog show or obedience trial people would come up to me with variations on one of two themes: "Everything that happened to you and Honeybear is happening to me. The same stuff." Or, "We were having so much trouble! I was discouraged and ready to quit. But your book has inspired me to keep going."

Late in 2004 Cheddar and I had shown in Open B for two days in Van Nuys, California. On Sunday afternoon we had packed up our stuff and were almost ready to leave when a woman came rushing over. "Aren't you Willard Bailey?"

"I've been accused of it."

"I'm reading your book, and I just want to tell you I have a golden retriever named Courage. We're just starting in Open. It's eerie. Everything that happened to you and Honeybear is happening to us. It's been so helpful to know we're not alone."

A year later I heard from her again. Cindy and Courage had gotten ten blue ribbons in Open A. Now they were starting in Utility A … and taking their lumps. "I'm carrying your book to shows," she told me, "it inspires me and helps me relax."

■ ■ ■

One spring morning in 2004 my phone rang. A woman's voice on the other end said, "Is this the Willard Bailey who wrote *Remembering to Breathe?*"

"One and the same," I replied.

"Bingo!" the voice said. Laura Asbill went on to introduce herself: "I live in Yorba Linda, California, and I'm president of the Skippy and Honeybear Fan Club."

"The what?!"

They were a group of Orange County residents, she explained. Folks who train dogs together at a Yorba Linda facility called Jump Start. At the time, most of them were Novice A people. They had read *Remembering to Breathe*, talked about it and coalesced into the Skippy and Honeybear Fan Club. There seemed to be about a dozen of them with breeds as diverse as golden retrievers, min pins, border terriers, and a Munsterlander. Laura was "mom" to a full-of-herself young golden named Belle.

She wanted to know when we might be showing in Southern California. The fan club wanted to meet Honeybear and me and host a dinner for us on Sunday evening after the shows were over.

Before we were able to accept their invitation, Honeybear died. Cheddar came out in Open B at Las Vegas six weeks later, stormed through three Open rings and finished his CDX in one weekend.

The end of our show year was rapidly approaching, and Laura let us know from time to time that they were eagerly anticipating our next foray into Southern California. I had shown Honeybear at Valley Hills Obedience Club a couple of times — in fact, she had finished her UD there. The Valley Hills trials would be held the first weekend in December in Van Nuys, not too far from Orange County.

Well, why not?

The fan club members were delighted. They immediately began planning what they assured us would be a gala weekend.

Meanwhile, the trial of the Southwest Obedience Club of Los Angeles (SWOC) was held on August 7. There's a special place in my heart for that club and that trial. It was there that I had entered OTCH-bound HB in Veterans just to get her comfortable again with the show atmosphere after she had missed eight months while recovering from her ruptured anterior cruciate ligament. And she had been magnificent, winning the class with a 198.5. Later she had shown in Veterans at SWOC two more times to go three for three with blue ribbons. I wasn't entered there in 2004. HB was too old and Cheddar wasn't ready for Utility.

A few days after the SWOC trial, here came the trial catalog in the mail. I was puzzled. Why would anyone be sending me a catalog from a show I hadn't entered? Leafing through it, I came across this full-page ad.

In Honor of:
Willard Bailey
&
Honeybear*

In celebration of your
accomplishments ... and
with thanks for your
contribution to the sport of
dog obedience competition
through the writing of:
Remembering to Breathe
From all the Novice A Teams past,
present and future
(just trying to remember to
breathe)

*OTCH Starbuc's Dream Come True UDX

Oh, that has to be the work of the fan club, I thought. And it was. Then, on the morning of September 1, I woke up for the first time in nearly 15 years without my big girl. As the first weekend in December drew closer, I began to have qualms about our visit with the Skippy and Honeybear Fan Club ... without Honeybear. On November 9, I sent an email to Laura:

We are really, really looking forward to the first weekend in December. That's something ultra-special, something I've never experienced before. But there is a downside. Someone very important will be missing.

Let's face it, all this is really about Honeybear. And she won't be there. In fact, just about everything in my life now emanates from the years with Honeybear — everything I write, all the training, all the showing, all my best friends (I checked it out; about 80 percent of my Christmas cards go to dog-related friends.) Bebop and Cheddar would not be here were it not for Honeybear. The house is filled with mementos from that fantastic adventure. Only my marriage to Barbara 45 years ago had an impact as great as the one Honeybear had. Which is why the story had to be told. So it's been a very difficult parting. I just hope I don't rain on the party at some point.

Laura emailed back that evening. What she said expressed beautifully what the Skippy and Honeybear Fan Club was about.

(We) have frequently mentioned HB's absence from our December meeting. We find ourselves second-guessing many little details. Her absence is like an A-bomb — can't be missed. She really has brought us together, and thanks to your book she will continue to give to others for years to come. So we will not dwell on her absence while not diminishing the gift of her presence.

We have all lost that one special dog, Willard, and that is the memory that flies through our minds when we think of your loss of HB. That's why we, strangers, cry so at the thought. We know the terrible pain; but then, there was the gift of her presence for so long. All that she taught you, and through your sharing her in your book, the way she touched our hearts as well.

To not rejoice over this first meeting of the Skippy and Honeybear Fan Club because she will be so missed would be a disservice to her. She was an awesome girl

*who exemplified the Golden spirit and the amazing
bond possible between man and dog.*

*She will sit quite silently at each of our meetings
and events ... and while none of us dares speak about
her too directly just yet, her presence will speak loud-
est of all.*

From the time Laura first contacted me, she periodically
sent me pictures of various parties involving club members and
friends. Parties for people's birthdays, for dogs' birthdays, the
annual dinner of Jump Start ... parties for the sake of parties.

Barbara would look at the pictures and say, "They sure know
how to throw a party."

And I'd reply, "What do you expect? That's Orange County."

Early December came, and off we went. What a weekend it was!
It started in Van Nuys, at the Valley Hills trials where Cheddar,
red-hot in Las Vegas, managed to flunk Open B both days. At the
trial, the official headquarters of the Skippy and Honeybear Fan
Club was a tent close to ours — but not too close; they were care-
ful to give us our space. A large yellow banner adorned the side
of their tent: "The Skippy and Honeybear Fan Club." In between
turns in the ring, we all sat around and talked dogs.

On Sunday afternoon we made the one-hour drive from Van
Nuys to Yorba Linda, where we discovered that our accommodations in a plush suites hotel were already paid for. That
evening we were guests at a candlelight dinner at Jump Start.
It was chilly and damp, but the partymeisters had prepared
for everything. Using tarps, they had turned an outdoor area
into an indoor dining room. Bundled up against the chill, we
had drinks, talked dogs and feasted on flank steak cooked to
perfection on a huge grill by Laura's son Josh, owner of a pro-
tection-trained German shepherd.

That was far from the end of it. On Monday Laura hosted a
brunch at her house. There, Dana Dacier (border terrier) gave

me a small stuffed honey bear. I named it Dana, and it became one of 2004's special Christmas tree ornaments — a memento of that wonderful weekend and its beautiful people.

After brunch a few of us walked our dogs through Laura's neighborhood. By then the members of the Skippy and Honeybear Fan Club had become warm and fuzzy, as comfortable as old shoes.

Following brunch, we were invited to Jump Start to watch the Monday afternoon classes. I ended up helping teach the Open obedience class.

All weekend I kept hoping HB was up there watching. It was all about her.

■ ■ ■

End of an era? Hardly. All those afternoons at Paradise Valley Park. All those tens of thousands of miles to and from shows. The unmitigated joy, the deep, dark gloom. The grinding road to the OTCH. And then those two years alone with the words and the paper. Hoping to create a book, then hoping some of the right people might enjoy it. But never dreaming it would impact people's lives.

On August 31, 2005, the one-year anniversary of HB's death, I received a card from Laura Asbill. It said, in part: "I know the world is still full of places she isn't. She continues to touch lives, warm hearts and inspire teams."

Somewhere Honeybear must know. She just has to. And she must be so proud.

Photo: David H. Smith

The dog who changed my life

■ Book Two ■

SUCH A LITTLE SPIRIT!

CHAPTER 1

The Little Guy

B ebop!
　　My little enigma in a border collie suit. The perfect dog. The perfect tragedian. I am writing this paragraph on the eve of my little guy's 12th birthday. What a ride it has been!

At the time Honeybear finished her OTCH, Bebop was 5½ years old. But I still referred to him as "the little guy." After all, he had been a new puppy when Honeybear was five and a seasoned obedience competition dog. He had gone along to the Gaines Classic that year and gotten his first view of big-time obedience competition from his vantage point inside a crate.

To me, Bebop never outgrew the diminutive designation "little guy." The notion of littleness became imbedded in my vocabulary about his training. He would do his "little go-outs." He was learning his "little recalls." We'd practice his "little scent articles."

In truth, he is anything but little. Standing 22 inches at the withers, weighing 48 pounds, he is good-sized for a border collie. And in the beginning at least, he was anything but a little guy in the obedience ring. But I'm getting ahead of my story.

■ ■ ■

My love affair with border collies had begun with Ott, the first border collie I remember seeing.

I met Ott when I was a student at Precision Canine, the obedience school where Honeybear and I were taking our first baby steps toward the Novice A ring. Ott belonged to Sandra Shults, an instructor at Precision Canine. Ott was a $50 dog that Sandra had acquired in Rice, Washington, before moving to Phoenix. Sandra had trained Ott largely out of a book, much of it done in the kitchen. I didn't know what kind of dog Ott was; I had to ask.

In those early classes, Ott was often a demo dog, and I found her riveting to watch. Waiting for Sandra to call her on the recall, Ott was a loaded gun about to go off. On the retrieve exercises, she would charge the dumbbell, snatch it up cleanly, charge back and sit in front of Sandra — eyes, ears, every fiber alert. Coming over the jump, she was sinewy grace and beauty. And the heeling ... locked in!

At a time when I was struggling to teach Honeybear attention, Ott *was* attention.

With the conclusion of every exercise, Ott got to play with her little blue-and-gold football, with Super Bowl intensity.

She quickly figured out that the treats were in my shirt pocket. If I dared sit on the floor of the training building, Ott was right there, nose deep in my pocket.

Before long I said to myself, "So this wiry black-and-white bundle of dynamite is called a border collie. What a neat dog!" The seed had been planted.

■ ■ ■

As Honeybear approached four years old, I decided I needed a second dog to be coming up behind her. Golden retriever or border collie? Border collie or golden retriever? Such a dilemma. And, oh, how I vacillated.

For a while I leaned toward getting a golden. I wheedled my way into picks of the litters of several of the top golden breeders in the United States. But each time, as the big day approached, I backed out.

Finally I put together a grand scheme. Karen Price had the best obedience golden of that era. I had driven to the Los Angeles area (Chatsworth) twice for lessons with Karen. I knew she was about to acquire another dog — pick of the litter from Sunfire Kennels in Connecticut.

So I proposed a plan that Karen accepted. On the morning she was scheduled to go to Connecticut, she would fly out of Los Angeles and I would fly out of Phoenix. We would meet at the Hartford airport, rent a vehicle and drive to Sunfire Kennels, somewhere in the nearby countryside. Karen would pick her puppy and help me select mine. What could be better than that?

Except that the night before we were scheduled to fly I couldn't sleep. Images of Ott — jumping, heeling, retrieving, playing with her little blue-and-gold football — filled my head.

At 5 A.M. I got up and called Karen. Then I called Barbara Biewer, the owner of Sunfire. "I'm sorry," I told each of them, "I've changed my mind." I could picture each of them rolling their eyes on the other end of the phone.

Ott had made me do it. And the die was cast.

■ CHAPTER 2 ■

Border Collies!

I f Ott planted the seed, a host of other border collies culti-
vated it.

Long before Honeybear had even finished her first obedience
title, her CD out of Novice A, I began hearing enthusiastic, glow-
ing things about "The Gaines," the pinnacle of dog obedience
competition in those days. The Gaines was a series of big-deal
tournaments — three regionals followed by a blowout event
called the Classic where those who had placed in the regionals
came together for a High Noon-like shootout to settle the whole
thing once and for all … until next year.

Honeybear and I were bumbling along, our pratfalls out-
numbering our little celebrations. But from time to time HB
would transcend my ineptitude and flash a hint of brilliance.
And once in a while that would prompt Sandra Shults or Debby
Boehm to take me aside and say, "Willard, if you ever get a
chance (Translation: If you and Honeybear can ever get your act
together enough to *qualify*), you should take HB to The Gaines.
It's an experience you'll never forget."

Gaines, Schmaines! I was still trying to figure out how to
heel my dog off-leash without wetting my pants. Still, I was
absorbing the message that there was something delectable out
there, and I wanted a taste of it.

By and by I learned that there would be a Gaines Cycle Western Regional in Denver in July of 1992.

"Let's go watch," I said to Barbara. "What a great chance to spend two days watching a whole bunch of the top obedience dogs in America."

So on July 24 we hopped on an America West flight to Denver. The event was being held in the Holiday Inn Convention Center. We checked in, quickly stashed our luggage in our hotel room and hurried downstairs to the show site. Everything was set up, ready for the next morning when the colors would be presented, the national anthem would be played, then the PA announcer would say, "Let the Gaines begin!" Words that in years to follow I would come to regard as the most electrifying sentence in the English language.

But on that first Friday afternoon it was simply the physical layout, the ambience that took my breath away. Six rings. Each with blue mats, white ring gates. Banners, table cloths, signs, everything decked out in the red-white-and-blue theme. And to think that tomorrow people and dogs who had started out just as HB and I had would be competing in those rings.

Looking back, I can pinpoint it. It was right there, on that very spot, at that very moment that I contracted "Gaines fever," a wonderful disease that would consume me for the next three years.

I spent the next two days lapping it up. And oh my! Of the 170 dogs entered, 67 were golden retrievers, 25 were border collies. I didn't know where to look first. But it was hard to take my eyes off the border collies. The beyond-belief dogs of Janice DeMello, Shauna Gourley, Helen Phillips. Fast, accurate, focused.

During that weekend in Denver, mantra-like, *I gotta have one of those* seized possession of my mind.

As we left Denver after that goose bump-inducing weekend, I was pumped, psyched about The Gaines. I vowed that someday soon Honeybear and I would make it to The Gaines. In Open.

I'm glad no one but Barbara was aware of that pie-in-the-sky pledge. They would have laughed out loud. Here I was with my green-as-grass Novice A golden. We had struggled mightily across 11 months of broken sits and downs to get our CD. We hadn't even shown in Open yet. And here I was with my sights set on the top competition in America.

Guess what! It didn't take us long.

■ CHAPTER 3 ■

Voodoo!

We came out in Open A in the fall of 1992, and my big girl finished her CDX in three shows. To qualify for a spot in Open at one of the Gaines Regionals, we needed three scores averaging 193 or better. Our three legs averaged 194. Voila!

The 1993 Gaines Central Regional would be held in San Antonio the first weekend in May. I entered and we went. I was proud of HB and, frankly, of me too. In our first pressure-packed taste of big-time competition, we failed to place by only the slimmest of margins — one of HB's paws landed out of bounds on the broad jump exercise.

The Gaines competition was actually three shows in one — the Red Show, White Show and Blue Show. Which meant each team showed three times in two days. For the first two runs the lead in our Open class was held by Kristina Pickering and her border collie Scout, from Las Vegas. Naturally I was transfixed.

Then, in their final run, Scout failed to sit on a halt during the heeling pattern, and they finished in sixth place. But Scout had clinched it for me. By the end of the year Honeybear would turn four. I had fallen head over heels in love with the sport. I needed another dog coming up behind HB ... and by God it was going to be a border collie!

I ran into Kris again in October at the Vegas Valley Dog Obedience Club's trial in Las Vegas. We said it simultaneously: "Hey, I remember you from The Gaines."

There were three days of trials. We had entered the first two, Friday and Saturday. We qualified on Friday but didn't place. We left before the awards were given out. As always, on Saturday morning we arrived at the show site before dawn. As we approached our tent, I said, "What's that sticking out from under our mat?"

It was two trophies. When we left early on Friday afternoon I hadn't realized that Honeybear had won awards for highest scoring golden retriever in Open and highest scoring golden in Friday's trial. When the awards were given out, Kris took them for us and secured them under our mat, to be discovered at dawn on Saturday morning.

■ ■ ■

As early as 1991, when Ott first burst into my consciousness, I had begun making occasional phone calls and keeping a file of notes and clippings. By the end of 1993 my search for just the right border collie was in high gear.

Naturally I was going to pick Kris Pickering's brain. Early in 1994 I had a long phone conversation with her. It was *the* seminal conversation in my search for a dog like Ott — and by that time a dog like Scout.

Kris went into detail about various types of temperaments one is apt to encounter in "BCs," as she called them. Then she told me about where I might go to get each of those types. She struck me as incredibly smart, detail-oriented, thorough. *No wonder she's a principal in one of the major law firms in Nevada*, I thought.

Eventually she said, "There's a guy in Montana who has wonderful border collies, Bill Berhow." She went on to tell me that Berhow had the top-ranked herding border collie in the United

States, Nick. *And* that Nick was a half brother of Scout's father, Jaff. *And* that Scout's mother, Jen, also belonged to Berhow.

By that time my ears were standing straight up. "Oh, I want to follow that up," I said. So Kris gave me the names and phone numbers of a couple of people who had Nick puppies. They, in turn, led me to Berhow himself.

Five days later, on January 25, I had Bill on the phone. I told him about Honeybear, and I explained that I was up to my eyeballs in obedience competition. I stressed that I was 6'5", which meant I wanted a tall border collie, one I could reach. "I've heard a lot of great things about Nick," I told him, "and I'm wondering about the chances of getting one of his puppies."

"Well, Nick is good-sized," he replied. "One of the bigger border collies, about 50 pounds. He breeds real typical to himself," Berhow said. "There's a lot of spirit in his offspring. They're very, very intelligent, very happy. And their temperament is what's made them such good dogs."

As it turned out, at the time of my call, Bill had a bitch there waiting to be bred. She had been shipped in from Mississippi, just across the state line from Memphis. I later learned that Berhow traveled all over the United States, trialing and conducting seminars. Attendees at those seminars saw Nick — the only dog to have won the United States Border Collie Association Herding Championship three times — then fell all over themselves, hustling to ship their bitches to Montana to be bred to Nick.

Jill, the bitch waiting to be bred to Nick, was a rough-coated dog, Berhow told me, from well-established herding lines overseas, but born in the United States. She was fairly good-sized for a female, he said, somewhat tall and long-built. "The pups would have every reason to be good-sized," he said.

I asked him about my chances of getting a puppy from that breeding. "Four or five of the pups are already spoken for," he said. "But talk to Jennifer (Howell), Jill's owner." And he gave me her phone number in Mississippi.

"Above all, I'm looking for a sound dog," I told him. Throughout Honeybear's career, we had been on needles and pins because she was mildly dysplastic in her left hip.

"When I get a female sent in for breeding," he assured me, "I ask that hips and eyes be checked."

"How are Nick's hips?" I asked.

"Nick is OFA[1] excellent," Bill Berhow replied.

That clinched it. We had known for a long time that Honeybear was mildly dysplastic in her left hip. And while it had yet to give us the slightest bit of trouble in her obedience career, it was always in the back of my mind. OFA excellents were few and far between, and to know that I had a shot at getting a puppy fathered by a superstar like Nick, and Nick had excellent hips … well, I was on cloud nine.

The next evening I was on the phone with Jennifer Howell. She was lavish in her praise of Nick. "He is one of the neatest border collies — one of the neatest dogs! — you'll ever see," she told me. "He has a super personality around dogs and people," she said. "And he's probably the best herding dog that's ever been in America. Bill and Nick have a record nobody else can even come close to."

She went on to describe Jill as a "super herding dog. A lot of eye. Sound temperament. Sweet. Eager to please. Submissive. Not an alpha dog at all."

On the other hand, she said, "Jill is real quiet and calm in the house. Just a nice dog to have around. But when she's around livestock it's a whole different story. She's intense."

"I understand Nick is OFA excellent," I said.

---

[1] The Orthopedic Foundation for Animals (OFA) reads X-rays and grades dogs' hips and elbows according to the presence and degree, if any, of abnormal development.

"Right!" Jennifer said, "he's the whole package. And Jill's hips are OFA good. Jill can go over a four-foot fence without touching it."

Jennifer also owned a Nick son, Sky. "And he can jump out of a six-foot run. I'll *guarantee* you the puppies will be able to jump."

All of which was music to my ears. I had this wonderful golden retriever, Honeybear, but I was haunted by the realization that her mildly dysplastic left hip was a ticking time bomb. One that could blow up in my face, ending HB's obedience career along with my hopes and dreams.

Now here I was, face to face with the puppy-acquisition opportunity of a lifetime. A son of the all-time United States border collie herding champion … with *excellent* hips. *And* whose mother-to-be was descended from not one, not two, but three international champions. *And* both dogs were on the large side, giving me an excellent chance of getting a dog I could reach. *And* both dogs had outstanding temperaments and lots of drive. That's called hitting a grand slam home run.

Berhow had told me that several of the puppies from the Nick/Jill litter were already spoken for.

Right, Jennifer said. Five were spoken for. All going to people she knew well. It broke down this way:

- The person Jennifer bought Jill from had first pick of the females. Jennifer would keep the second female pick. Someone else had a third pick. That left me in fourth place if I wanted a female. Which I didn't. What I wanted was a little Nick.
- On the male side, Bill Berhow had first pick. "I know Jennifer doesn't have a lot of money," Bill told me early on, "so I agreed to take a first-pick male puppy in lieu of a stud fee." The second-pick male was already spoken for. Which left me in third place for a male. But who cared? The whole litter had to be pure gold.

Jennifer wasn't taking deposits. We'd wait until the litter was on the ground, then sort it out. "Keep in touch," she said.

Which I did, probably to the point of making a pest of myself. On January 31 Jennifer told me that Jill had been bred twice, that morning and two days earlier. Let's see, that should put the puppies on the ground by April 4. So I settled in to wait.

Well, "settled" isn't exactly the right word. I was like a cat on a hot tin roof. Barring some lousy luck, I was about to get my border collie. A puppy sired by the greatest herding border collie in American history. And in all likelihood a *sound* dog.

Jennifer and I talked from time to time. It became clear that if I was flexible, if I'd accept either a male or a female, I had a pretty good chance of getting a puppy. Well, maybe … but what I really wanted was a little Nick. Then, early in March, she made my day, my month, my year, when she said, "I talked to Bill Berhow this morning. He said, 'I don't need another dog right now. Let Willard have my first pick male.'"

I thought I had died and gone to heaven. First-pick male from a dream litter!

The puppies were born on March 31, a few days earlier than we had anticipated. Four females and two males. All robust and healthy — and I was in the driver's seat!

My fundraising consulting business was taking me around the country a bit, and I had accumulated a bundle of frequent flier miles on Delta Airlines. I had enough miles for one round trip coach flight and two round trips in the first-class cabin. And now was the time to use them.

I couldn't wait to see the puppies. Jennifer and I agreed that somewhere around five weeks would be the perfect time. By then they'd look more like little dogs than black-and-white rats. Jennifer worked weekdays. She was a draftsman at an architectural firm near where she lived. So we agreed that May 7, a Saturday, would work.

Although I had yet to see him, I had named my puppy — or thought I had. Voodoo! As I write this, I can't recall precisely how I arrived at that name. The logic probably went something like this: My puppy would be coming from Mississippi where voodoo is still practiced. (Never mind that Louisiana is more of a voodoo state; Mississippi was close enough.) Voodoo is all tied up in magic, black magic. My puppy would be mostly black, and surely he'd be magic.

You say all that's a stretch? Never mind! Well before dawn on May 7, 1994, I was at Phoenix Sky Harbor International Airport, waiting to board Delta 1270 for my first look at Voodoo!

■ CHAPTER 4 ■

The Shoelace Shredders

I planned my schedule so as to accomplish my mission and sleep in my own bed that same night. Everything went like clockwork. After changing planes in Dallas, I arrived in Memphis at 3:30.

Once I've described myself, I'm easy to recognize. At the top of the jetway, an attractive thirtysomething woman stepped forward, smiled and said, "Willard Bailey?" It was Jennifer. Soon we were in her car, on our way to Cockrum, Mississippi, a 30-minute drive.

Jennifer had already told me she lived in the boonies' boonies. Cockrum was so small it almost didn't exist. Her postal address was Hernando. We drove through countryside distinguished by sharecroppers' farms. A country road led to a narrower country road. Which led to a lane. Down that lane was Jennifer's small farm … and *my puppy!*

The house was tiny, dwarfed by the barn behind it. It had been a sharecropper's house, Jennifer told me. Her friends from the architectural firm where she worked had helped her redo it — air conditioning, hardwood floors, new kitchen and bathroom fixtures. But the original tin roof remained, and I wondered what that roof did for her electric bills in the Mississippi summers.

We pulled in, got out of the car, and I stepped into ... mud! It had rained that morning and the night before, and the whole place was one mud. A condition I hadn't considered when I wore a pair of nearly new bone-colored Rockport shoes.

We slogged directly to the barn. Jennifer had the puppies in a chain-link pen with wood chips on the floor. Six little black-and-white bouncing, tumbling balls of fur. And one of them was going to share a wonderful adventure with me.

I opened the gate and shuffled in, not raising my feet lest I step on one of them. They immediately attacked my shoelaces. One at a time I picked them up. Let them snuggle against my chest. Petted soft heads. Endured needle-like teeth digging into my fingers. Loved tiny pink tongues licking my face while an army of five ravaged my shoelaces.

Four girls and two boys. Each had a name. The smaller of the boys was Petey. The larger (*so* Mississippi) was Bubba.

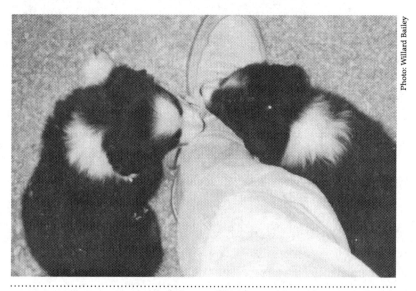

Photo: Willard Bailey

The shoelace shredders

Now it was time to hold the boys. First Petey. Cute. Soft. OK. Then Bubba. But first I had to pry him off my right shoestring. Bubba had this big, wide hourglass blaze of white on his head and face. The hourglass narrowed in the middle of his face. Two dark eyes were set in the coal-black fur on either side. His chest was white. All four legs terminated in white boots.

Bubba? Nah! This wasn't any Bubba. But not a Voodoo, either. All that could be decided later. Bubba, Schmubba! Voodoo, Schmoodoo! What he was was *mine*.

I said nothing. The puppies were only five weeks old. I'd be back in two weeks to pick up whatizname. A lot could change in two weeks. But it must have been obvious; I kept going back to Bubba, picking him up, nuzzling his nose with mine.

"I'll make a final decision when I come back," I told Jennifer as we drove to the Memphis airport that evening. "Well, I think I already know," she said with a smile. "And there are several ranchers around here who wish you'd decide you don't want a puppy; they are drooling over Bubba."

I arrived back in Phoenix at 11:30. Barbara met me at the airport. "Well?" she said.

"My God, they've named him Bubba," I replied.

Well, it was a cinch no border collie of mine was going to be a Bubba. And the one I had secretly picked wasn't going to be a Voodoo, either. There was nothing dark and sinister about that little guy — only a penchant for wreaking havoc with my shoelaces.

What, then?

Jennifer's little farm and her kennel went by the name Berihill. So his registered name should start there. And I wanted something upbeat, befitting a border collie, something jazzy. That was it! Berihill's Mississippi Jazz Man. And his call name would emanate from that.

■ ■ ■

MAY 21, 1994

Two weeks from the day I had mucked around in the Mississippi mud and gotten my shoestrings shredded, I was back on Delta Airlines again. This time Barbara was with me, and this time we were in the first-class cabin. Remember those two frequent flier tickets? Their time had come.

We flew into Memphis, rented a car, drove several miles into Mississippi and spent the night in a Holiday Inn. By mid-morning on Sunday we were pulling into Berihill Farms. Jennifer had the two males waiting in a pen in the living room of her tiny home. I didn't hesitate a moment. I walked over to the pen, bent down, picked up the puppy with the beautiful white blaze and said, "Hi, Bebop. Oh, what an adventure you and I are going to have together."

The adventure began sooner than I had anticipated. While Petey remained in the pen, Barbara and I took turns hugging Bebop. Then we put him on the floor.

It was a beautiful Mississippi spring morning, and we had left the front door open. Bebop spied that open front door, took off down the front steps and headed straight for four sheep that were grazing in the front yard. All of us jumped up and tore after him. I made a dive and caught him just short of the sheep. "Oh God," Jennifer gasped, "those sheep are mean, they would have killed him."

Just before we arrived at the airport we stopped at Wendy's for lunch. I took "the Bopster," as he would come to be known, for his first walk. He peed but didn't poop.

Soon we boarded our Delta flight and were on our way home. Theoretically my little guy would spend the next several hours in the Sherpa bag under the seat in front of me. Those were the rules. The reality was the flight attendants took one look at him and declared that he could be on my lap except when meals were being served or during landing.

Bebop quickly became the darling of the first-class cabin. Everyone had to ooh and aah, pet him and hold him. "This is the world's next great obedience competition dog," I told them.

We had to change planes in Dallas. There was just enough time to take Bebop outside on his brand-new leash. "Outside" at the Dallas airport consisted of steep hillsides covered with ivy. I set Bebop down. The ivy came up to his shoulders. *Well, this dog hasn't pooped since I picked him up,* I thought, *and it's going to be a long time until we get to Phoenix.* So we walked through the shoulder-high ivy. Nothing. We walked some more. Nothing. Finally it was time to board our flight to Phoenix, so I scooped him up. Mission not accomplished.

Another flight, another first-class cabin. Same result. Bebop was the star of the cabin.

Photo: Willard Bailey

Bebop at five weeks, with Jennifer

Back in Phoenix, we claimed our luggage in a hurry, got my van out of the parking garage, then prepared to head home. Bebop was in the Sherpa bag. As we were about to leave the airport, Barbara said, "You know, I should have stopped in the bathroom while we were in the terminal." So we circled the terminal and I parked at the curb while Barbara dashed inside.

Pretty soon my nose told me that something had gone wrong in the Sherpa bag. Sure enough! Bebop wouldn't go in the airport ivy, but he had just let fly in the bag.

So my little guy rode to his new home wrapped in a towel on Barbara's lap. When we got home, the bag went into the washer and Bebop's rear end got scrubbed.

■ ■ ■

Before long it was time for Bebop's supper, his first meal in his new home. He was in his two-foot by three-foot wire pen, the pen all of our puppies have started in, back as far as I can remember. Jennifer had given me a small bag of Science Diet puppy chow, the food Bebop had been eating in Mississippi. Now I put it in a small bowl, knelt next to the pen, held the bowl by my face and said, "Watch me." When the tiny black face with the wide white blaze looked up at me, I placed the bowl on the floor of the pen.

That was Bebop's first obedience lesson. The beginning of a lifelong — well, at least career-long — focus on focus. How is the dog going to know what you want him to do, much less attain the precision necessary to excel in competition obedience, if he isn't paying attention to you?

My new puppy spent his first night at our house, and many nights thereafter, in the wire pen at my side of the bed. It was his first night ever away from the warmth of his littermates, so he wimpered a few times, but I reached down and reassured him. He quickly went back to sleep.

And so it began.

CHAPTER 5

Little Puppy Games

My little guy was only seven weeks old, so his obedience training began with little things. Little puppy games. Little exercises cunningly designed to convince Bebop that I was the most exciting, most fun thing in his tiny world. Indeed, that I *was* his world.

I used a lot of AnneMarie Silverton's puppy exercises. We began with sessions as short as he was young — maybe 30 seconds a few times a day. We'd work up to ten minutes at a pop by the time he reached six months.

I'd sit on the kitchen floor, feet against the base of the counter, legs spread to form a V. I'd hold him by his collar, and toss a little ball or a small toy toward my feet. Then I'd rev him up: "Look at that! Do you want it? Do you want it?" Bebop would strain into his collar for a few seconds, then I'd say, "Get it!" and release him. He'd run to the ball.

Border collies are not natural retrievers, so the first few times he got to the ball he'd stand over it or start to push it around with his nose. He didn't know what to do with it. So I'd get on my knees, crawl to him, say, "Get it!" put the ball in his mouth and back up, gently pulling him forward by the collar, all the while saying, "Bring it to me."

We'd do that about three times, twice a day. By the third day a light bulb went on in that fuzzy little head. *Aha! Bring ball back, get treat.* He also quickly realized there was no way he could take possession of the treat until he surrendered the object that was occupying his mouth. I parlayed that into the next step: He didn't get the treat unless the ball was surrendered into my hand, not dropped at my feet.

Within a few days, he had learned to retrieve. And once he had it, *boy he had it!* He was like something possessed. Years later, if a dumbbell went under the ring gates when I tossed it in practice, coming to rest a few feet outside the ring, he'd leap over the top, fetch it and return. Once, when it was only a few inches outside but just out of reach of his long nose, he rooted with such power that he knocked down the entire end of the ring.

"Such intensity!" people would say. I can't remember when the first time my inner response was, *Yeah, too intense?*

A few days after he joined our family, I bought a softball-sized fleece ball, tied it to a long string and let him tear around the backyard trying to catch it. Great exercise and great fun.

As we played our little puppy games, the objective foremost on my mind was *focus.* I wanted Bebop's attention glued to me to the exclusion of anything or anyone else, no matter what.

The little guy was my first border collie and it would take me awhile to realize that border collies come with built-in capacity to lock on, attention-wise, and not let go. Kris Pickering, during one of our earliest conversations, had laughed and said, "Border collies are great if you can stand having a dog sit and stare at you all day."

How true! Don't ever try to stare down a border collie.

Our focus on focus began the morning after Bebop arrived at his new home here in Phoenix. I'd sit on the floor with the Bopster between my legs, facing me, in close, my hand in his collar. I'd hold the food between my teeth and I'd say, "Look!" as I pointed to my mouth. Then, "Get it!" as I popped him up to get the food. He quickly learned to focus on my face when he was in front of me — head up, all eager expectation. I progressed to spitting the food ... and for a long time watching it bounce off his nose and forehead. Never mind, he knew where the treats were coming from, and he locked in on my face. Eventually I began to gradually — maybe six inches at a time — work my way up to a full standing position. Have you ever tried, for any length of time, to stand a quarter of the way up or a third of the way up? That's cruel and unusual punishment for the legs and back.

Which was OK, for all the while I could picture us on the blue mats at The Gaines, competing in Super Dog, in hot pursuit of that gold dumbbell. No pain, no gain.

Bebop and I both loved our little follow games. In the beginning the lure was quite blatant. I'd cradle a treat in the crevice between the thumb and forefinger of my left hand. Bebop could see it and smell it, but he couldn't quite get it. With the dog at

Photo: Barbara Bailey

Home sweet home

my left side to start, I'd cup my hand over his muzzle so he could nibble at it, and we'd move a few steps before I let him have the prize. At that point the objective of the exercise was to let him know the food was there and to let him know that if he moved with it he'd soon get it.

Before long, I'd shift the food to a conspicuous position between my thumb and forefinger. I'd hold the treat a few inches over his head, directly between his eyes. We'd move out slowly in straight lines, big circles left and right, and in little figure eights between and around my legs.

I'm 6'5" and my little guy's head was less than a foot off the floor. One more challenge for the legs and back. But no matter, my puppy was taking the baby steps that would one day lead to precision heeling on the blue mats as he dazzled at The Gaines.

Those little follow games also served to teach him to get ready to heel. I use the word "place" to get my dogs to swing into heel position, set to go. It was a seamless transition from our straight lines, wide circles and little figure eights to swinging into heel position next to my left leg.

"Place," I'd say as I positioned the treat a few inches above that imaginary bull's-eye on his forehead. Then I'd rotate my left hand and arm to lure him into heel position. At that point I didn't care whether he finished standing or sitting. When he arrived at a point where my pants seam was between his eye and his ear, he received lots of praise and the treat he had been following.

Bebop loved puppy recalls, a two-person exercise. Someone would kneel down and hold him, positioned between her forearms, hands clasped across his chest. I'd *run* away, about 50 feet, sink to my knees and yell, "Bebop, come!" The little guy would have been struggling as I ran away. Now the holder would loosen her grip enough to allow him to vault over her hands. He'd come flying to me, right up my chest. And from that position he could give my face a bath with his little pink tongue.

The leaping start was one more touch to help build drive and a speedy recall. As if this kamikaze puppy needed any more drive. Time would reveal that what Bebop needed was a *drive-reduction* program.

I also immediately began to teach him to tug — with rope toys, tennis balls and, above all, on the leash.

Why on the leash? Because the leash is always there when I'm training. Attached to the dog's collar, in my pocket or hanging around my neck. With that in mind, I have my leashes made at a local tack shop, from lead rope. And my training leashes have no loop handle. Instead they have a knot, just something I can grasp. Or nothing at all. I've seen dogs run, dragging a short leash, and catch a hind leg in the handle. I don't need that.

There is this wives' tale that is endorsed in many puppy classes: "Don't ever tug with your dog, it'll make him vicious."

Nonsense!

What *is* important is that you control the game. Which means what? It means *you* decide when the game starts, when the dog releases the tug object and when the game ends. Most importantly, tugging must not be about possessiveness. It must not turn into a battle where the dog is threatened by your efforts to "steal" his toy and decides that by God he must protect it. That said, tugging is a wonderful way to engage Fluffy in interactive play and stimulate bonding.

So my first step with Bebop was to teach him to release, on command, whatever he had in his mouth — a ball, a rope toy, the leash ... my sock. That involved a simple exchange, a treat for a toy. He learned that in one day.

Then we got down to the main event. And it was at that point that the intensity I had first seen as he learned to retrieve exploded into the one characteristic that would most define him for the rest of his life. When my puppy — not yet nine weeks old — tugged it was like World War III. He dug in hard with his back feet. He thrashed. He flailed. If I raised the toy, Bebop came up with it, dangling a few feet off the ground, teeth bared, hanging on for all he was worth.

But at the point where I said, "Enough!" World War III ended abruptly. He'd drop the toy, leash, whatever, and go into his border collie crouch, every fiber of his little furry black-and-white being intent on what I had in my hand. I'd wait a few seconds. Then: "Get it!" And he'd explode upward. World War III was underway again.

There was more than near-pathological intensity involved. It was at that point that I began saying to people, "Feel the muscle on the back of this dog's neck." They would, and their response would be, "Whoo!" Pound for pound, Bebop turned out to be the most powerful dog I've ever known.

■ ■ ■

Initially most of our training, our little adventures, took place in private. I have a dilemma that I wrestle with each time I have a new puppy.

My dogs are headed for the obedience competition ring. I want them well socialized. They are going to spend their lives in close proximity to other dogs and legions of people. I want them comfortable in the presence of those dogs and people. Not afraid. Not skittish. Certainly not aggressive. Friendly but not so distracted they can't focus on the task at hand.

Some of those people — ranging from veterinarians to judges — are going to want to or need to put their hands on my dogs. I want to mold a puppy who isn't going to shy away when the obedience judge approaches to do the exam part of the stand for examination.

In other words, I want to nurture a dog who is prepared to cope with the world. Who will delight in the great adventure that is to follow. That means the puppy cannot be raised like a hothouse flower.

All of which takes on added importance when the puppy is a herding breed — a border collie, for instance. Herding breeds, unless well socialized as puppies, can become shy, skittish, the antithesis of what you want an obedience competition dog to be. Which means you gotta get them out there.

But until they receive their final immunization shots at about 16 weeks, puppies are vulnerable, at risk of contracting parvovirus, distemper, parainfluenza, hepatitis, and heaven knows what else.

Several years ago Dr. Toben said, "I see people carrying tiny puppies into PetSmart and I cringe. No telling what they can pick up in an environment like that."

I've weighed all of this, and I err on the side of caution. Until my little guys have had all their shots, I avoid places where other dogs congregate — PetSmart, parks, training sites and the like. Dead dogs aren't very well socialized.

Instead I go to shopping centers, terminals at the airport, places where there are lots of people without high risk of infection. I also invite selected people and dogs in to see my puppy. People and dogs I know are likely to be disease-free.

■ CHAPTER 6 ■

Thunderbolt Moments

Particularly after you've survived the scary adventure of training your first dog, the training journey becomes a blur. Sure, you have a plan, but mostly it's putting one foot in front of the other, day after day after day. Some find it boring. I never have. But it *is* a process of tiny steps, and the critical incidents, the thunderbolt moments, are few and far between.

One that hit me right between the eyes came sometime in the summer of 1994. Bebop must have been about three months old. I was talking on the phone with Helen Phillips. By the time I was beginning to train Bebop, Helen had already attained the role of icon in the world of dog obedience. A sage, a wellspring of good common sense about dog training. And best of all, she's always been delighted to share the wisdom she's accumulated during more than 40 years in dog sports.

Anyhow, one summer afternoon I'm talking with Helen about Bebop and his training. And the conversation turns to bonding. By that time I understood the crucial importance of bonding as it applied to a successful obedience competition team. And Helen says, "Willard, would Bebop rather play with you or with Honeybear?"

I didn't know the answer, and it was one of those electrifying moments that I'll never forget.

I agonized over the question and its implications. The consensus among many of America's top obedience competition trainers is that a new puppy who is destined for top-level obedience competition should have only limited access to any other dogs in the household. In fact, many would have advised crating my little guy for several months, letting him out only to interact with me.

The point of Helen's question was to make me think about whether I was Bebop's world or just another somewhat interesting two-legged object in a world full of fun things — the most fun being Honeybear.

It wasn't that I hadn't thought about play. It wasn't that I hadn't thought about how Bebop and Honeybear would relate when the activity was play. But much of that thought, much of my planning, had been focused on one toy, the *ball*.

The idea was that I should take Bebop out in the backyard *alone*, no HB. The likely scenario would be that I'd throw the ball and Bebop would run over to investigate. He'd sniff it, not know what to do with it, either stand over it or walk away. If Honeybear, a ball-crazy golden, was out there, she'd swoop in, pick it up, spirit it away and probably be quite possessive about it, at least as far as Bebop would be concerned. Which would say to Bebop, *the ball is something I can't ever have.* And right away he'd turn off of ballplaying.

So the idea was I'd throw the ball, run after it, compete with Bebop, make the ball a lot of fun, get him excited about it. That was the game plan.

OK, on a warm summer day out into the backyard we go, just Bebop and me. HB's inside, her nose plastered against the window. I throw the ball. Bebop tears after it, grabs it, runs back to me chomping furiously. So much for working hard to teach my puppy to play ball. Lesson over!

By and by out came ball-crazy HB. I threw the ball. Both dogs tore after it. Bebop snatched it, ran it by Honeybear as if to say, "Ha! Ha! Look what I've got." Then brought it to me. Honeybear never had a chance. Not the first time, not the one-thousandth time. Not any time in between. Bebop was, after all, a border collie.

It was matters of that sort that occupied me when I considered the relationship between the two dogs. Aside from such consideration, Bebop and Honeybear had free rein.

And it was because of that free rein that Helen's question frightened me. Had I blown the whole thing? Fortunately my fears were unfounded. What Bebop wanted Honeybear to do was tug. Honeybear had never learned to tug and she sure wasn't about to take lessons from this rambunctious black-and-white whippersnapper.

Besides, HB only had eyes for me. Throughout her life she steadfastly refused to give a hoot about any other being, be they two-legged or four-legged. Many was the time, at an obedience trial, that I would ask Barbara to hold HB on leash while I spent 60 seconds in the port-a-john. The uproar that would ensue was embarrassing. I could put her on a down or a sit out there and she'd be fine. But the idea of being forced to stay with someone else — anybody — was more than she could handle.

So I was lucky, I guess, that aside from a few occasions when HB condescended to a brief spurt of play, what she most wanted was for Bebop to go away.

CHAPTER 7

"Slow It Down!"

By mid-summer the Bopster had finished his puppy immunizations and was ready to explode upon the world. Tuesday evenings found us at Sunshine School for Dogs, a puppy kindergarten reputed to be the best in the Valley of the Sun. Of course my little guy was well into his training, but there were 12 other dogs in the class, making for his first opportunity to focus on me and perform in the presence of a bunch of other dogs and handlers. Each session was preceded by 10 minutes of free play, Bebop's first chance to get down and dirty with other dogs since he had left his littermates.

The class was oriented toward pet obedience — lots of hands-on manipulation of the little guys, and staples such as come, down, sit, stay, and walk on leash. There was also a smattering of watch-me attention — important for where we were headed. Mostly, Bebop benefitted from the socialization.

He graduated with top honors. How could he not? He already knew most of it before we attended the first class. His primary role across those seven summer Tuesday evenings was that of demo dog.

Then, on August 11, his competition obedience training got into high gear. I took him to Debby Boehm for his first private lesson. On that afternoon he shared a private lesson with Honeybear. Under Debby's guidance, HB and I worked for half an hour while Bebop watched from a crate. Then Bebop took center stage while HB watched.

In retrospect, the significance of the dynamics operating in the environment at that time was lost on me. And remained lost on me until recently — more than a decade after it was over.

I guess I had blinders on, so to speak, as I trained HB, and I had my head down as I started my young border collie. The relationship between those two separate but simultaneous training endeavors never entered my mind … until I began working on this book. Until I sat down with Debby to discuss the early days of Bebop's training. What did she remember?

Nearly the first words out of her mouth went right to the heart of what had somehow escaped me for so long. And now I see it.

From time to time I hear someone in dog sports say, "Every dog is different." How trite is that? But it's exactly the point.

Honeybear was my Novice A dog. Honeybear was a best friend. Together we went all the way to an OTCH. Beyond that — far beyond that! — Honeybear was the dog who changed my life.

But, in training and more so in the competition ring, HB wasn't exactly shot from a gun. Small wonder. At the very outset, in a parks department beginners class, she was force-trained. Koehler methodology, misapplied. There was no joy in those training sessions. She was jerked around a lot before she was five months old, and she never got over it. All that changed when we began training with Debby, but HB didn't have the foundation of want-to that might have come from a more motivational beginning.

And it didn't help that for most of her career she was saddled with a boring teammate. It took me a long time to shed my inhibitions and actively focus on becoming the most fun thing in her world. I became Honeybear's cheerleader, and I cheer-led her all the way to an OTCH.

Now here came Bebop. A border collie — *all* border collie. The word that best describes Bebop's response in training and competition is *explosive!* Motivated? He was *driven!*

On that August afternoon in 1994, when Honeybear and Bebop showed up together for the first time at Debby's training facility, HB was not quite five years old and approaching the prime of her career. She had been to the Gaines Central Regional in San Antonio the year before and had missed placing in Open by only the width of a paw. Now we had qualified for the Gaines Classic in Pasadena, the ultimate tournament. In less than 90 days we'd be on those blue mats, duking it out with not only the best but the best of the best in America.

Fired up? I was *manic!* And I was well on my way to getting HB plenty fired up, too. And that state of fervor wasn't about to end. About the time I was satiated with Gaines tournaments — a year later when we finally placed at the Western Regional in Salt Lake City — we embarked on an OTCH quest, and the passion intensified.

Looking back 11 years later, Debby pointed out that I had this off-the-wall young border collie and I was perpetually in cheerleading mode.

HB had a tendency to lag. Bebop insisted on forging and wrapping. Honeybear might wander off and sniff between exercises. Bebop would spin off my leg between exercises, run in tight circles around me, jump up on my back.

I'd throw the dumbbell. Honeybear would trot out, gently pick it up and trot back. Bebop would charge out, sometimes hit the dumbbell so hard it flew out of the ring. Or he'd snatch it up and charge back chomping on it so hard I would fear for my fingers when I reached down to take it.

Yet Bebop was the dog, Debby pointed out as we reminisced, that I was constantly juicing up. Why hadn't she pointed it out way back then? Well, she had, until she was blue in the face.

But I was in my manic training state. Anything with four legs that crossed my path got cheer-led.

On that long-ago August 11, I was oblivious to all that. I was excited, more manic than usual. It was my little guy's first lesson with Debby. The first of many enroute to the blue mats in Super Dog at The Gaines.

That afternoon we started him on little left-hand finishes. "Slow it down, Willard," Debby said more than once that afternoon. She helped me refine my hand position on his little follow exercises, which by that time had progressed to little heeling exercises.

And he did his first little go-outs. I had brought a little white porcelain dish. We put it on the floor against a side wall. I'd drop a treat into the dish, back up three feet, say, "Away!" and send him. At first he was leery of the dish. He'd run to it, jump back, move to the side, lunge again.

"Whew! That bowl is pretty tricky," Debby said.

Driving home that afternoon, I was ecstatic. Bebop's first little lesson with Debby! He was on his way.

After that we had a private lesson once a week. During those sessions I took notes. Often Debby wrote notes. I have two loose-leaf notebooks, each about three inches thick, crammed with notes from those lessons. They provide a detailed history of Bebop's progress, or lack of it.

Looking back, it is well-documented that right from the get-go we saw signs of problems that would haunt us throughout Bebop's career.

SLOW IT DOWN! in big bold letters, appears every few pages. I had a tendency to let Bebop set the pace … and he was a border collie. Not only that, a *driven* border collie. And the more I let him drive, the more wound up he got.

My notes reveal that Debby was constantly cautioning me not to let him flare his butt out. "Freeze," she'd say. "Tell him to get back, and don't move until he does." That was the beginning of his persistent insistence on wrapping around in front of me as we heeled.

"Slow down," was not part of Bebop's vocabulary. Keeping him in heel position rather than allowing him to jump out half a body length was an ongoing battle, one I never won. Debby grew hoarse saying, "You must not let him out front, looking back. Keep him back in heel position!"

Fat chance.

And when it was time to *wait* for some reason, the poor little guy almost came out of his shiny black coat. Right from the beginning he didn't want to sit all the way. As he agonized through his wait for the recall, his butt was up an inch or two, rarin' to go. That would come back to haunt us in a major way in Novice B.

Well, I had wanted a shot-from-a-gun, driven border collie. I sure had one. And I could not have been happier.

Trouble was, I was feeding into it. In practice, when he'd complete an exercise, I'd explode into excited praise, as had become my custom with HB. Which only served to goose an already over-the-top dog.

Sure he forged. Sure he wrapped. Sure he anticipated. Sure he ran around me in tight circles, spun and jumped on my back between exercises. But those were "border collie things," annoying, frustrating add-ons that in no way detracted from the raw brilliance of this dog.

Bebop was lightning fast. His learning curve was headed right through the roof. Attention? He never took his eyes off of me.

Super Dog, here we come!

In fact, Bebop did go to The Gaines that fall. Just not as a competitor.

Honeybear and I had qualified for the Classic in Pasadena. The Classic was the culmination of the Gaines year. By November the three regionals had been held. The winners of the three divisions were automatically invited to the Classic. The rest of us could qualify by submitting three scores averaging 195 or better in the division we wished to enter. HB and I did.

Not only would it be a second opportunity for us to place in Open (we didn't), it would give me a chance to let Bebop soak up the unique atmosphere of a Gaines tournament in a noncompetitive, fun way.

Which he did. On November 18, the day we arrived and were setting up, I walked my little guy around the rings, let him sniff the edges of the blue mats. We played a little ball at ringside. Over and over I said things like, "Get used to this, little guy. Someday you and I are going to be in there."

We stayed on one of the top floors of the Pasadena Hilton, the host hotel. The Pacific Obedience Association, the local organization that was staging the event, had set up the "Potty Zone," a place to pee and poop your dog at one end of the hotel garage's lower level.

Getting from our room to the Potty Zone offered a two-pronged learning experience for Bebop. It began with an elevator ride, his first. It ended with a flight of open stairs, also a first. Although those stairs were both open and clangy-sounding metal, scary at first, by the second day my little daredevil was bounding up and down.

During the Classic, they announced the schedule for the 1995 tournaments. The Western Regional would be held at the Salt Palace Convention Center in Salt Lake City on August 13 and 14. "Honeybear," I said, "we've got work to do. There are less than nine months until the regional."

■ ■ ■

The upcoming nine months, I knew, would be an endless string of perfect afternoons — Honeybear, Bebop and me alone on the Polo Field at Paradise Valley Park, our favorite place on Earth. HB and I would be working to get ready for our big weekend in Salt Lake City. Bebop would be one year old the end of March, and he was nowhere near ready to enter the competition ring. It was obvious he was bursting with potential, and I wasn't going to rush him. When his time came, I wanted him good and ready. I wanted him to burst upon the scene.

So 1995 looked like a year of smoothing and polishing. Smoothing out Bebop's rough edges to get him ready for the Novice ring. Getting HB shined up to sparkle in Open at the Western Regional.

■ CHAPTER 8 ■

"My Champion"

As Bebop approached his first birthday, everyone was marveling at what a handsome guy I had. With his wide white blaze, his broad white chest, his snow-white muzzle, and his white stockings, all offset by a shiny black coat, he was, in a word, gorgeous. And he was a lot of dog: 22 inches at the withers, heavily muscled, pound for pound the most powerful dog I've ever known.

When I got him, border collies were still in the American Kennel Club's (AKC) miscellaneous group. That meant they could show in AKC obedience trials and earn obedience titles. They could also compete in the conformation ring but were limited to the miscellaneous class with no opportunity to earn championship points. That was fine with me; obedience was the only thing on my mind.

There were, however, rumblings that eventually the border collie would be accepted into the herding group. Which led to a heated political brouhaha between those who were pushing for full acceptance of the breed by the AKC and those who were dead set against it. The frothing-at-the-mouth vehemence of the latter group stemmed from their concern that exposure of the border collie to the breed ring would lead to breeding for "pretty" rather than all the qualities that had for centuries combined to make the border collie the world's premier herding dog.

I watched the donnybrook with, at most, detached interest.

Eventually the pro-AKC faction won, and by early 1995 it had become official that the border collie would become eligible for full-recognition status in the herding group on October 1 of that year. That meant border collies could compete for championship points in the conformation ring.

Bebop was not yet a year old, but more and more I had been looking at my handsome young guy and saying to myself, *Wow, if ever a dog was cut out to be a breed champion ... !* Not that I had a clue. Not that I had ever heard the words *breed standard*. I hadn't even stood outside a conformation ring and watched the judging. My dog show world had been obedience. Period.

Sandra Shults, Ott's "mom," showed her own dogs in the breed ring and occasionally — mostly as a favor — showed friends' dogs. One evening, as Bebop approached his first birthday, Barbara and I were standing in the kitchen, talking about what a fine specimen he was turning out to be. I said, "I've been thinking about asking Sandra if she'd be willing to show Bebop in the breed ring."

There was a silence for a moment, then a small voice from the other side of the room said, "I might like to do that."

I guess my answer was, "You?" Barbara had been very supportive of my obedience endeavors. She had helped when Honeybear and I were training. At dog shows, she had brought our lunch and videotaped our ring appearances. But she hadn't spent one minute in any sort of hands-on competitive role with a dog. So for a moment I was taken aback. Then I thought, *That would really be neat.* So I said, "Why not? Let's do it."

Debby Boehm was the leading competition obedience instructor in the community. She was in the process of taking Honeybear and me all the way to an OTCH. But common wisdom in the community had it that she was an even better conformation handling teacher. Barbara enrolled in a handling class. One morning Debby came over to our house and took Barbara through the whole drill of bathing and grooming Bebop to get him ready for the show ring.

Most evenings found us at a nearby park, practicing down and backs, big circles, stacking, baiting, and the rest of the show ring presentation essentials — usually underneath the street lights. I knew precious little about it, but I quickly picked up enough to tell Barbara what I was seeing and help her a bit.

The practice sessions continued through the brutal heat of the Phoenix summer. Barbara usually returned home exhausted and put cold compresses on her forehead.

Bebop's membership in the herding group became official on October 1. Barbara and her big handsome guy were ready, and they walked into the conformation ring for the first time at Kachina Kennel Club on October 29.

Barbara and I added breadth and depth to the word "green," and to "clueless" as well. Barbara had done her preparation diligently. Those exhausting summer evenings paid off. She handled the little guy well, moved him smoothly about the ring, presented him to his best advantage — and immediately began walking out of the ring with ribbons.

Trouble was, we had no idea what she had won. What did *reserve* mean? How about *best of winners? Winners dog? Best of opposite sex?* So we'd hurry home. Barbara would call Debby, tell her the color of the ribbon and read what it said. Debby would tell her what Bebop had won. Then we'd rejoice.

There was plenty to rejoice about. In my naiveté, I had thought my big, strong, handsome guy looked every bit the part of a champion. As it turned out, judges seemed to agree.

In their first show, with Barbara quaking in her boots, Bebop took best of breed. As well he should have; he was the only border collie entered in conformation that morning.

Two weeks later, Arizona White Mountain Kennel Club, Scottsdale Dog Fanciers Association and Sahuaro State Kennel Club combined forces to stage a three-show weekend at WestWorld of Scottsdale. Multi-show weekends tend to attract lots of entries. This time Bebop had some competition.

On Friday, as Barbara and the Bopster headed for the ring, I headed for a hiding place, a spot where I wouldn't distract Bebop but could still watch the proceedings. I found that amusing, for Barbara had hidden each time I had shown Honeybear in Novice A.

I was some distance from the ring, but I saw that Barbara and Bebop returned to the ring several times to repeat their presentation. I figured that must be good.

Finally they came running back to us — Barbara with a handful of ribbons, Bebop with best of breed and his first point. Same drill on Saturday, and another point.

Sunday figured to be interesting. At the time, Bebop and I were in Debby's Thursday morning obedience class. When Barbara was about to bring Bebop out in conformation, Debby called me one day. "Willard, there's something I thought you'd like to know," she said. "You know that lady in the Thursday morning class with the Malinois?"

I had to think for a minute. "Vaguely," I answered. How could I be focused on who else was in the class? I had to spend every second trying to keep up with my little spinning, leaping maniac.

"Well," she continued, "a couple of weeks ago she said to me, 'My, that certainly is a handsome border collie in our class!'"

I allowed as how that was nice.

Then Debby said, "I'm telling you this because she's a breed judge, she judges herding breeds, and she's going to be Bebop's judge at Sahuaro State Kennel Club in November."

"Oh!"

Sunday was that day, and her admiration for my little guy had not abated. He took best of breed for his third point.

And so it went. Bebop and Barbara showed 16 times. Bebop took best of breed 11 times and best of opposite sex once. Not that it was all tra-la and a walk in the park.

The following March (1996) Barbara had Bebop entered in the Superstition Kennel Club shows in Mesa. Barbara has a long history of sinus infections — nasty things that pound in various areas of her face and head.

On Saturday she was experiencing mild pain in the forehead area just above her eyes. That day Bebop took best of breed under Dr. Carmen Battaglia, one of the most prominent, most respected AKC judges.

On Sunday morning she got up with throbbing pain, so severe she had trouble seeing. I suggested we stay home. Barbara wouldn't hear of it. On the way to the show she put her head back and closed her eyes. Occasionally she'd moan and say, "Oh God, it's just pounding."

We set up the grooming table in our tent. I lifted Bebop onto the table and Barbara went to work — the final fussing and primping that every handler does for an eternity right before going into the ring. Her head continued to throb. Her vision was drastically curtailed. As we got closer to ring time, several times she put the brush down and said, "I don't know if I can do this."

Each time I replied with something like, "This is no good. Why don't we just pack up and go home?"

"No, no, we'll do it," was always the answer. When it came time for them to go into the ring, off they went.

That morning's hiding place was some distance from the ring, and I couldn't see a whole lot. Only that they were doing their thing and that they returned to the ring a time or two to do it again.

Finally it was over. As Barbara and Bebop returned to the tent, I could see she was almost in tears. "All that running," she gasped. "My head's just BEATING!" Then she said, "When it was time to run him around in a circle, I got out there and I couldn't see the judge. I just hung on to the leash and Bebop took me back. Bless him!"

That was the day the Bopster took best of opposite sex.

Their roll continued. By early July they had nine points. You need 15 for a championship. But you also need two majors for a championship. A major is 3, 4 or 5 points at a show. So all Bebop needed was two three-point majors.

Fat chance. Majors in the border collies ring were tough to find. Our part of the United States is by no means a hotbed of herding. Few border collies were showing in conformation in an area with a radius of several hundred miles.

The Prescott shows were coming up in mid-September. Prescott, I knew, was one of the least likely places for Barbara and Bebop to find a major. More likely, Bebop would be the only border collie entered in conformation there that weekend. When the premium list arrived early in August, I knew that one way or another — still seeking our UD or starting on our UDX — Honeybear and I would be entered in obedience in Prescott. I encouraged Barbara to enter Bebop in the breed ring. "Regardless of how the entry turns out," I told her, "showing under a real judge for two days will be good practice for both of you."

She entered.

When our judging program arrived in the mail ten days before the shows, I was stunned. "Look at this, Barbara," I said, wanting her to affirm what my disbelieving eyes were telling me. "Two dogs and four bitches both days. That's a three-point major each day."

There were Bebop's majors, waiting in the most unlikely of places. But who were the other dogs and where on earth were they from?

Dick and Kay Guetzloff had moved to Arizona from Palatine, Illinois, several years earlier, bringing with them reputations as two of America's foremost obedience trainers and competitors. They had not disappointed. Indeed, they had dominated Arizona obedience competition from the day they arrived. And their presence and willingness to help others had raised the level of competition competence in the state significantly.

By late 1996, Dick had become a friend. A few days before the Prescott shows, Dick said to me, "We rented two of those spots down by the equipment shed." He was referring to a tiny fenced area close to the obedience rings. An area with four spaces that had been sold as preferred parking. "We're only going to use one of them," he continued. "If you and Barbara would like to use the second one, you're welcome to it."

Wow, would we! The show area in Pioneer Park was a broad, flat expanse of green grass, perfect for obedience. But it was in a bowl at the bottom of a steep hill. You parked on top and had to haul your stuff down to ringside the day before the show, then pull it all back up when the show was over on Sunday afternoon. Traipsing up and down that hill with a heavy cart was a royal pain. So we thanked Dick and parked next to their van.

On Saturday morning, the first day of the shows, Barbara hustled over to the conformation area to purchase a catalog. "OK, who are they?" I called out as she returned, before she could even get back into the tent.

"Wait'll you see," she replied as she handed me the catalog. I looked. My mouth dropped open.

Dick and Kay Guetzloff were as smart as any exhibitors who ever walked into an obedience ring. They never failed to see and seize every advantage. And Kay, who had been in obedience for 30 years, had jumped into conformation with her border collies in 1996. After all, her already prolific and successful breeding program, Heelalong Border Collies, would be enhanced if her OTCH-disposed dogs also carried breed championships.

So Kay, also looking for majors, had stacked the deck at the 1996 Prescott shows. Of the six dogs entered, four were owned by Dick and Kay. The fifth, bred by Kay, was owned by Sandy Beeler of Queen Creek, Arizona. Kay had asked Sandy to enter her bitch. As a result, the entry had one dog named Bebop and five called Heelalong This-or-That.

With all those dogs entered both days, the Guetzloffs had reasoned, how could they fail to take home a major with a dog from the Heelalong line at least one of the two days? They had better. It had cost them a tidy sum to enter all those dogs.

We saw it a bit differently. Bebop was a fine specimen of everything a border collie was meant to be: big, strong, bred to work. Plus, he was quite a handsome guy. He had seldom lost across the 11 months he had been showing.

The Guetzloffs also had fine dogs, but nothing to strike terror into Barbara's heart. We, too, saw opportunity beckoning.

Again, at ring time I stayed my distance. Barbara described the scene as "Kayotic." Kay was running in and out of the ring trying to show four dogs, all the time yelling at Dick to do this and that.

When it was all over, when the tumult and the shouting had died, the judge, Helen Miller Fisher, pointed to Bebop. And Barbara went back to the motel with yet another best of breed and Bebop's first major. Now they had 12 points and needed only tomorrow's major to finish his championship.

Have you ever bathed a dog in a Motel 6 at 10 P.M.? If you're a conformation person you have. If you aren't, don't even think about it. There were sopping wet towels (ours, not the motel's) everywhere. And what do you do with them if the motel doesn't have a dryer? (A large plastic bag in the back of the van, that's what. And when you get home the next day you have this heavy, soggy mess.)

So I'm in the shower with the Bopster, soaping and rinsing. Special shampoo, you understand, to make his whites whiter. Then Barbara has him on the grooming table, blow-drying and brushing and trimming. And pretty soon it's past midnight and we have to get up at 4 A.M.

I showed Honeybear in Open B and Utility B the next morning, and I can't even remember being in the ring. We must have flunked both classes; the AKC has no record of our even being alive that day. I haven't a clue how we blew it.

Never mind, this day was for Barbara and Bebop.

Shortly after 12:45 that afternoon I hid behind a tree and Barbara pranced Bebop into the ring of Judge Dorothy McNulty. The woman was ancient (many breed judges are) and Barbara said later she was concerned the judge might fall asleep during judging.

The tenor of the whole class was different on Sunday. Dick and Kay had gotten their act together and there was less "Kayos."

While I was hiding behind the tree, about a dozen of our "doggie friends" gathered in the area outside the ring. The word had spread; they knew what was at stake. Suddenly I realized Merrelyn Clark was standing next to me. She was the judge who had been in class with Bebop and me at Precision Canine, and had put Bebop up as best of breed at the Sahuaro State show. And now, in Prescott, we were peering around opposite sides of the same tree on the afternoon of afternoons. "This is it," I told her. "If they get this major today, she finishes him."

"I know," Merrelyn said. And there was a pride in her voice when she continued, "I was one of the first."

It seemed like an eternity. Kay kept running all those dogs in and out. But finally, when the big moment came, the judge didn't even hesitate. She pointed to Bebop, and Barbara got the blue ribbon.

Indeed the judge had not fallen asleep in the ring, and Bebop became the first border collie breed champion in Arizona.

As Barbara and her new champion emerged from the ring, they were mobbed by well-wishers — screaming, clapping, hugging. In the middle of it all, Bebop slipped away from her and there were a few calls of, "Loose dog!" But not to worry. He wasn't going anywhere, he was coming to me.

Dick and Kay walked by. Kay said, "Congratulations, Barbara." Dick tipped his trademark black hat and said, "Congratulations." Then he looked at me, grinned and said, "Send money."

Some friends we were. First we accept their parking space, then we clean their clocks two days in a row.

Later that afternoon Barbara went shopping among the vendors' tents. She came back with a red plush squeaky toy in the shape of a star for her new champion. "Because he was a star today," she said.

■ ■ ■

Shortly after she left the ring that memorable Sunday afternoon in Prescott, Barbara handed me the leash and said, "Here, you can have your dog back." Then almost immediately began referring to Bebop as "my champion."

What a metamorphosis! My desire to get another dog had not exactly been met with open-armed jubilation at home.

At the time, we had two dogs and a cat. Honeybear, at four, was flying high, competing in national tournaments, having a blast. Barbara's toy poodle, Smittie, was nearing the end but still very much with us. Squeakie, our cat, had marched in our front door in the fall of 1988 and would rule the roost for another 11 years.

The first border collie breed champion in Arizona

Barbara would shake her head and say, "We don't *need* another dog!" Besides, she had seen several border collies and they had not impressed her. She often referred to them as "those slinky things."

Then there was the proposed gender of my next dog. I wanted a male; I thought he'd give me more drive (refer back to the whole cheer-leading thing with HB). But going back 40 years, there had never been a male animal in a Bailey household. My mother's dogs, cockers Inky and Soot and miniature poodle Joy had been females. So had the dogs Barbara and I had owned: Tiffany and Smittie, toy poodles; Ginger, a Sheltie; and of course Honeybear. So a male puppy would be quite a break with tradition. Nevertheless, I had seen the future, and it had balls.

Finally there was Karyn, our next-door neighbor. Across the 24 years we've been neighbors, she's had several dogs. Yet she knows zilch about dogs. Long ago we learned to discount down to zero anything Karyn said about dogs.

When she learned I was looking for a male border collie, her mantra for several months was, "A male! He'll lift his leg and pee all over your furniture!"

So we headed into the latter stages of the acquisition of Bebop with Barbara repeating, "ANOTHER dog?! A *male?!* A *border collie,* one of those slinky things?!" And Karyn babbling, "A male?! He's going to pee all over your furniture!"

By and by my little third dog/male/border collie puppy who would surely pee all over the furniture arrived. On the second day Barbara exclaimed, "Oh look! When I pet him, he leans in." And on the third day she said, "When I kiss him on the forehead he snuggles up — he's a love!"

A few months later we decided to take some pictures. Not that that was anything new. Any inventory of the pictures of our dogs would be recorded in tonnage. Most often, though, those pictures show just the dogs or the dogs with me. Barbara is the photographer in the Bailey household. Long ago we agreed that a camera should not be placed in my hands.

But on this day, for reasons long since forgotten, the "shoot" would feature Barbara, Bebop and Bebop's framed pedigree. Which placed the camera in my hands.

The idea was that Barbara would kneel by the flower bed. Bebop would sit at her side. Barbara would place one arm around Bebop and proudly display his pedigree with the other hand.

That's not quite how it turned out. The photo that's blown up, framed and hanging in a prominent spot in our house shows Bebop wrapped around the front of Barbara, frantically licking her ear. She's hugging him with her left arm while gamely holding the pedigree out front with her right hand.

That photograph represents a relationship that has developed into one of the world's great love affairs.

■ ■ ■

The phone call came from Cincinnati in the wee hours of the morning on July 21, 1996. We were sound asleep and didn't even hear it ring. Barbara got the message the next morning. Her mother had suffered a heart attack and died before the paramedics arrived. It was a devastating blow; Barbara had been unusually close to her mother. Whenever her mother visited they would spend a lot of time together, often in the kitchen cooking.

A couple of weeks after the funeral Barbara was in the kitchen preparing dinner. It was one of those evenings when her mother's death hit her hard. Working at the sink, she began to cry; I had not yet gotten home. After a couple of minutes she became aware that someone else was behind her crying. She turned around. It was Bebop.

Leaning against the sink, she slid down and sat on the floor. Bebop came over and put his chin on her shoulder, his face

Photo: Willard Bailey

The beginning of a love affair

against her face. He cried and she cried. After a while he moved to her other shoulder and they cried some more.

Privately over the years, Barbara has admitted, "Bebop is my all-time favorite dog." Never one to miss the opportunity to get a little dig in, I've often reminded her: "But you kept saying, 'Another dog?! A male?! *A border collie?!*'"

To which she has always replied, "But I didn't know it was Bebop."

And, of course, not once has he lifted his leg and peed on the furniture.

CHAPTER 9

"Get Outta My Face!"

Bebop's conformation career may have been illustrious while he was in the ring, but it was hair-raising at ringside. Soon after Barbara began taking him to practice matches, it became clear that he didn't want another dog in his face. When an approaching dog got within six feet, Bebop's hackles went up. At about three feet, Bebop showed the other dog what pretty white teeth he had. And at a foot he lunged, snarled and snapped. Not once has he laid a tooth on another dog, but he sure has scared the bejesus out of a few of them.

Bebop wasn't always like that. At Sunshine School for Dogs, at four months of age, he roughhoused with the other young dogs and never showed the slightest hint of aggression.

I believe it was an acquired behavior, and I can pinpoint the day it happened. He must have been about six months old. Every morning I would take him to a nearby park, throw a tennis ball and let him chase it. He loved those sessions.

One morning, out of nowhere, three stray dogs materialized and came running over. They didn't seem aggressive. I made the mistake of throwing the ball, certain Bebop could outrun them. That isn't what happened. One of the strays got the ball, and when Bebop ran over to try and steal it back — in play, I'm certain — all three dogs ganged up on him. I broke it up right away, nobody got hurt and I chased the strays out of the park.

But I'm sure the incident left its mark on Bebop. From that day forward, he was afraid of strange dogs.

When Barbara got him into a congested situation, that became a problem. At a large dog show where you have many conformation rings side by side, there can be dozens of dogs and handlers crammed together. Worse, many of those handlers will be klatching with one another while their dogs wander around uncontrolled at the end of the leash.

That was where it got most dicey with Bebop. Waiting to go into the ring, Barbara would clasp him around his chest, holding him close, restraining him from lunging should he be incited by another dog wandering into his space. The whole scene was unnerving for her.

Bebop won best of breed 11 times, making him eligible to come back and show again in the herding group showdown in

Honeybear, Barbara, Bebop

Photo: Jack Cody, Sr.

the afternoon. Another traumatic experience. Veteran handlers — particularly the professionals who dominate conformation — sensing Barbara and Bebop were rookies, unseasoned, would crowd them from behind as they ran in a circle around the ring. That made Bebop nervous, concerned about the dog crowding him from behind. He'd turn instead of gaiting, and more than once he turned and gave the dog who was crowding him a warning snap.

It didn't take Barbara long to learn to hate groups. And to stop going. "There's no reason to go," she said. "All it does is upset him and condition him to be skittish about the breed ring. Besides, no judge is going to put up a border collie to represent the herding group in best of show."

That was true. The border collie was the new kid on the block in the AKC. There wasn't even an established breed standard for border collies. Most judges didn't know what they were looking for when they judged the breed. Debby and others had been telling Barbara, "The first judge who puts up a border collie from the herding group is going to get run out of town."

So Bebop would do his thing in the morning, get his customary best of breed, then we'd go home.

By the time I brought him out in obedience I was well aware that he didn't want another dog in his face. I stayed alert and found that it wasn't difficult to steer him away from possible confrontations.

I can remember only one incident, and it was good for a few laughs. Friends of ours had bouviers, one of whom, a big male named Max, was the most titled bouvier in the history of the breed. During an obedience trial at WestWorld of Scottsdale, Max's owners went to get a hamburger. They accidently left the door of Max's crate slightly ajar. I was walking Bebop when Max sauntered over, right into Bebop's face. Bebop dispatched him in short order, and Max set a new world record for the 50-yard dash.

Perhaps the most troubling aspect of Bebop's aversion to getting up close and personal with strange dogs was the doubts it raised in our minds. What would happen, we wondered, if we introduced a new puppy into our household?

We found out in 1996.

CHAPTER 10

Mom

Smittie, Barbara's toy poodle, died in 1995 at the ripe old age of 15. Smittie had been a great little dog, and Barbara was heartbroken. "I don't ever want another dog," she said. "This is too painful." That lasted about a year. Eventually Barbara decided it might be nice to have a poodle puppy again. And she wanted one that was robust, sturdy, full of life.

With her birthday coming up in March, I did some research. The right breeder seemed to be Judy Wilson in Snowflake, Arizona, about 165 miles northeast of Phoenix. And she was expecting a litter about March 24. On March 20, a note in a small box informed Barbara that we'd go "puppying." She could pick out a toy poodle.

Before Barbara got Smittie, she wanted a chocolate poodle. Indeed, Smittie had started out chocolate ... then turned silver about a year later. Barbara still had chocolate on her mind, so when she opened her birthday present she immediately said, "I want a chocolate poo." OK, we'd try again.

Judy Wilson's litter, born March 24, was coal black. Nevertheless, her reputation, the reputation of her litters, was excellent, so we decided we better drive up to Snowflake and take a look.

On May 30, Barbara, Honeybear, Bebop, and I piled into my Chevy Suburban and off we went. By that time the litter was almost 10 weeks old, and Judy had one puppy left.

By and large, those who purchase puppies from Judy Wilson have their sights set on the conformation ring. The puppy that was left had long legs and seemed destined to exceed the breed standard for toys, no more than 10 inches at the shoulders.

Barbara had told the breeder she was looking for a dog with plenty of spunk. Judy described the remaining puppy as "feisty, fearless and very sweet."

Long story short: Chocolate, schmocolate, we walked out of there that afternoon with a coal black bundle of fluff. Barbara would later name her Noché, Spanish for night.

Bebop and Honeybear had waited in the Suburban. As we started down the driveway, they were in the back seat, I was driving, Barbara was in the right front seat with Noché snuggled in her lap. Before we were out of the Wilsons' driveway, Bebop reached around the back of Barbara's seat and gave Noché a big kiss.

So much for our concerns about how Bebop would react to a new dog being introduced into the household.

And it went a lot farther than that. When we arrived home, everybody entered the house through the kitchen door that opens into the garage. Barbara put her new puppy down on the floor. The first thing Noché did was run to Honeybear and bite all four paws. Noché and HB did not get off to a wonderful start. And it never improved. At best, Honeybear regarded Noché as a little pest that had to be tolerated. At worst, well ...

Noché pestered Honeybear constantly. One evening not too long after Noché joined our household they were in the kitchen. HB was busy begging at the sink as Barbara fixed dinner. Noché was engaged in one of her favorite games, grabbing Honeybear's tail and tugging. Finally HB had enough. She spun and snapped at Noché, not even laying a tooth on her. But Noché, startled, shrieked as if she had been killed.

In a split second, Bebop came roaring from the other side of the house, right into HB's face, all teeth showing. What he said was, "Honeybear, don't you ever do that again!"

Honeybear did do it again about a week later, with the same result; Bebop scolded Honeybear in no uncertain terms.

It was at that point that we began to call Bebop "Mom," and we became aware that he was raising Noché: checking her over from head to toe daily, teaching her to play and protecting her.

As the years rolled by, Noché, at nine pounds, established her role as one who wanted no crap from any other dog who happened to be in the house. Or anywhere else, for that matter; Noché has never seen a Rottweiler she couldn't lick. The exception is Bebop. As I write this, he's 12 and Noché is 10. He's still "Mom." He can do anything he wants at any time; Noché is still his "puppy."

I have a theory about that, but no way of validating it. When Bebop left Mississippi, his litter was seven weeks old. The last time he saw his littermates they were about the same size Noché was the day we picked her up in Snowflake. And they were black. Perhaps he viewed her as one of his littermates and was delighted to be reunited.

CHAPTER 11

The Capriciousness of His Fuzzy Black Butt

As Bebop finished his conformation title, Barbara went back to sandwiches and videotape. And it was time to focus full time on his obedience career.

It was obvious my little guy was ready to burst upon the obedience competition world. He knew the Novice exercises cold. Man, could that dog heel! And talk about attention! When we were working, his eyes were glued to me; he was undistractable. In fact, he has spent his life at home looking back over his shoulder at me and bonking his head on chairs, tables, whatever is in his path.

Best of all, nothing, including food, brought him as much pure joy as working with me. Bebop was — and now, at age 12, still is — the epitome of want-to. Too much so, time would reveal.

He would be three years old in March, so yes it was high time he began his competition career. And what better place to bring him out in Novice B than the spring trials at Phoenix Field and Obedience Club (PFOC) at Pierce Park. I had a warm, soft spot in my heart for that place and those trials. It was there, six years earlier, that I had wobbled, scared to death, into the ring for the first time with Honeybear to begin the most fulfilling adventure of my life. So we entered.

Our first judge, on Saturday, February 22, was William Oxandale, the man who had written the book on judging. Bebop did not disappoint, but his score of 197 wasn't quite enough for a blue ribbon. Dorothy Holmes and her Rottweiler Dancer scored a 198 to win the class.

On Sunday morning Bebop again was steady and accurate. Under Judge Carl Friedrich, our run seemed to be going well. The final exercise was the recall. After he said, "Exercise finished," the judge walked over to the end of the ring where Bebop and I had just finished our run. "I have to tell you this because you couldn't see it," he said. "When you left him to walk to this end of the ring, he picked up his butt about this far," and he showed me about two inches between his thumb and forefinger. "Then he put it back down."

I must have had the look of death about me, for he quickly continued, "No, I didn't NQ you, I took off three points." He paused briefly, then he said, "But those were the only points I deducted this morning."

Oh!!! We had just missed a perfect score by the capriciousness of my little guy's fuzzy black butt.

Kay Guetzloff had been watching at ringside. She had seen my exchange with the judge at the far end of the ring. "Did he zero you?" she yelled as we left the ring.

"No," I replied, "we just blew a 200." Of course, we still had to do sits and downs, but Bebop was like money in the bank on the group exercises. We ended up with another 197, second again to Dorothy and Dancer's 198. But hey, nearly a 200 in only the little guy's second time in an AKC ring.

Clearly, I thought, we were headed for the brilliant obedience career I had envisioned as I brought Bebop home from Mississippi. Visions of Super Dog danced in my head as we drove home that afternoon.

The Bopster wasted no time finishing his Novice title. We showed again the following Saturday at Superstition Kennel Club. Under one of my favorite judges, Nancy Pollock, we scored a 196.

In all, Bebop showed eight times in Novice B, placing first or second six times and averaging 196. He was definitely on his way.

■ CHAPTER 12 ■

"I'm Going to Ruin Your Day"

Shortly after Bebop turned two, it was time to have him OFA'd.

The Orthopedic Foundation for Animals (OFA) grades dogs' hips and elbows according to the presence (if any) and degree of dysplasticity (abnormal development). The X-rays are taken locally and sent to the foundation in Columbia, Missouri. There, three veterinary radiologists independently read the X-rays and arrive at a consensus. The dog's owner is then notified. A dog cannot be OFA'd until he is two years old.

I had been licking my chops over this. After all, Bebop's father, Nick, was OFA excellent. His mother, Jill, was OFA good. And Bebop was a great little athlete. So I made an appointment at Apollo Animal Hospital and took Bebop in fasting, just in case my little wild man would need to be anesthetized. Dr. Mark Trueblood did the exam.

When I returned to pick up my dog, Dr. Trueblood beckoned me into an examining room, saying, "Willard, I'm going to ruin your day." I didn't have to be a veterinarian to interpret what I saw on the viewing board. Bebop's right hip was no thing of anatomical beauty. The socket was shallow, the ball at the end of the femur was flat and somewhat square. And there were arthritic changes in the joint.

His left hip looked good and his elbows were perfect, but there was trouble in that right hip. We sent the radiograph off to the OFA to see where they would place that ugly-looking hip on their scale of bad news. The report graded Bebop's right hip *moderately dysplastic*.

Bummer! But we'd wait and see. Honeybear was mildly dysplastic and her condition had yet to manifest itself. She jumped effortlessly.

I had hoped someday to breed Bebop; he was such a magnificent guy — so pretty, so strong, and such a sweet boy. But no way, now. Before long we had him neutered.

How could this be? Bebop was a son of a sire who was OFA excellent and a dam who was OFA good. "You just never, never know," I kept saying. "You get a puppy and no matter how much due diligence you've done, it's a crap shoot."

■ ■ ■

When Bebop was still a puppy, as soon as he completed his immunization shots, I began taking him to matches and shows. Not to go into the ring, just to be there, to socialize, to sop up the show atmosphere and get comfortable in that environment.

He was such a beautiful puppy, so cute, so friendly, that he attracted a lot of attention. People would gravitate to us and want to know where I got him. I would proudly tell them about his heritage, that he was a son of the premier American herding dog of our time.

Those who knew herding would ooh and aah. Inevitably the next question would be, "Are you going to do herding with him?"

"No," I'd reply, "I got him strictly for obedience and we're going to focus on that."

Honeybear was showing often in Open B at that time — polishing, polishing, hot after a Gaines placement. Bebop would always go with us and we'd always find a remote place on the show grounds to play an intense, all-out game of ball.

In the spring of 1997, HB and I were entered in the obedience trials of the Superstition Kennel Club, held on the campus of Mesa Community College. Just to the west of the obedience rings was a large grassy multipurpose field. Empty and waiting. At noon, when the obedience rings were temporarily shut down for lunch, I took Bebop out into that empty field for a bonkers game of ball. He'd tear after it — in those days he was the fastest thing west of the African veldt — snatch it up and come hustling back, mouthing it furiously. We'd fight over it for half a minute or so. Then I'd say, "Give." He'd place it in the palm of my hand and go into his classic border collie crouch, every fiber of his being at ready, waiting for me to throw it again.

As we played that morning, I was vaguely aware of a man in a wheelchair watching us, first at a distance, then rolling a bit closer. When we were finished and heading back to our tent, he intercepted us. Smiling, he said, "That dog's got a lotta eye, where'd you get him?"

I knew next to nothing about herding, but I was vaguely aware that "a lotta eye" was a good thing. It had something to do with a border collie's ability to stare down the sheep, intimidate them and move them. I knew that it was one of the characteristics that made the border collie the world's best herding dog.

"Do you know much about herding?" I asked the man in the wheelchair. He allowed as how he did. "Do you know who Bill Berhow is?" I asked.

"I sure do," he replied, and he leaned forward to get a better look at the dog who had attracted his attention. We talked for a few minutes and he allowed as how my dog came from a mighty fine daddy. As we parted, he shook his head and said, "That puppy of yours sure has a lot of eye."

That brief encounter stuck in my mind. Who was that friendly man in the wheelchair? He seemed to know a lot about herding. And he seemed quite impressed that I had a Nick puppy. By and by I was with a group of people who regularly entered their border collies in herding trials. I asked them if they knew anything about a herding guy in a wheelchair. I had hardly gotten the word *wheelchair* out of my mouth when they chorused, "That's Joe Escobar!" They went on to tell me that he was one of the better herding trialists in Arizona. That he also gave herding lessons and conducted herding seminars.

"All from the wheelchair?" I asked, astounded.

"You bet," they assured me. "He's really good."

My exchange with Escobar, as well as a few other conversations with herding types who seemed either nonplussed or disappointed when they learned that Bebop's future would be in obedience, not herding, left me uneasy. *Maybe,* I thought, *I should at least expose him to sheep, to see what happened.*

That simmered for a few months. Then I learned about a woman in Buckeye, in the far southwest part of our Valley of the Sun, who had won top honors for having the best herding border collie in the United States the previous year. (Nick, by that time, was getting old and fat and was fading fast.) Her name was Dodie Green, and I learned she had been in the top echelon of herding trialists for many years.

I wondered, *would she … ?*

So I got her phone number and called her. She said she'd be happy to set an appointment. Bebop and I would go down to her place some evening, she'd introduce us to herding and evaluate Bebop. Of course I told her about Bebop's father. And I told her about the unfortunate OFA outcome. "That came as such a surprise," I said, "particularly considering that Nick is OFA excellent."

There was a long silence on the other end of the line. Finally Dodie Green said, "Willard, Nick is not OFA excellent. Nick has never even been OFA'd."

"But Bill Berhow told the breeder that Nick is OFA excellent," I said.

"Have you ever seen the OFA certificate?" she asked.

"No," I admitted. Then I remembered. Jennifer had said something about Berhow telling her he had lost the paperwork. In the excitement about getting a Nick puppy, that had flown right by me; I hadn't given it another thought.

"Bill goes around the country giving herding seminars. People see Nick and want to breed their bitches to him. There are Nick puppies all over the United States ... and the dog's never been OFA'd," Dodie said.

At the time, I did nothing. I didn't even call Jennifer. What *could* I do? Jennifer was as much a victim as I was. Berhow was allegedly running around the country lying. Exactly what action could I take against him? I could get involved in a big, expensive brouhaha that would sap my time — my training time, the most precious time I have — and net me nothing. And in the final analysis, exactly whose fault was it that I had not more carefully done my due diligence before I bought a puppy whose daddy had never been OFA'd?

Besides, Bebop was manifesting no ill effects of that ugly hip — or, more to the point, none that I recognized at the time. And we had work to do. Hip, schmip, my little guy was headed for Super Dog, and it was important that we focus on that.

■ CHAPTER 13 ■

The Great Entertainer

With Honeybear, I had experienced all the anxieties that come with training your first obedience competition dog. My training was fear-driven — no, fear-*inhibited*. We trained for Novice, got our CD, then and only then began learning the Open exercises. I was afraid if I trained the advanced exercises while I was training Honeybear for Novice, I'd confuse her and the whole thing would end up a big mess.

By the time my little guy came along, I had gotten over all that. You'll recall that during Bebop's first lesson with Debby we started teaching him go-outs. I put a treat in a little dish and sent him away from me a couple of feet to get the treat out of the dish. Never mind that he was afraid of the dish.

The result was that on the day he finished his CD he was well on his way to being ready for the Open ring. In fact, I could have brought him out right away and probably qualified. But I had my sights set on Super Dog. And he had shown in Novice that he had the right stuff. Bebop had tremendous talent, scary potential. So he finished out the month of March kicking fuzzy butts in Novice. Then he vanished from competition for seven months while we polished.

It paid off. He came back in October and showed only three times in Open A to cakewalk to three blue ribbons and his Companion Dog Excellent (CDX) title. Super Dog, here we come!

Once Bebop got into Open, he became an instant crowd pleaser. Not only was he fast and accurate, he radiated intensity, exuded want-to. And if I heard it once, I heard it a hundred times: "Willard, you've got to start to get control of that dog between exercises." Fat chance! When he heard, "Exercise finished," he exploded out of heel position. Spinning, running around me in tight circles, jumping on my back as I walked to the starting point for the next exercise.

But when it was time to begin the next exercise, I'd say, "Place!" and he'd fly into perfect heel position, head up, eyes locked on mine. Focus personified. Those at ringside loved it.

Debby, however, wasn't too fond of it. She had perennially bad knees, and they had recently gotten worse. During our lessons, between exercises Bebop was a whirling dervish. Which struck terror into Debby. "Keep him away from my legs," she'd say, jumping back. "I don't want to have knee surgery."

"He's not going to come to you," I'd respond.

"He's going to take me out as he spins off of you," she'd reply.

Indeed, he almost did take out a judge. We were in Shirley Indelicato's ring at an obedience trial put on by Sahuaro State Kennel Club. As we finished one exercise and headed for the starting point of another, Bebop's antics were in high gear. Shirley made the mistake of stepping toward me to say something, only to jump back as Bebop's rear end flew by her legs.

"Oh my," she said, "he almost got me."

After we had finished and I had my little maniac on leash but had not left the ring, she tried again: "What I started to tell you before was, look, you've drawn the largest crowd; there's hardly anybody watching the other rings. Bebop's quite an entertainer."

I had been so focused on my little guy that I hadn't noticed. But yes, they were two and three deep outside our ring. Nearly everyone at the obedience trial had gathered to watch my zany but gifted young border collie.

It was at that point that I began calling Bebop "The Great Entertainer."

By the time we finished Bebop's CDX, Barbara's little champion had had quite a run in obedience competition. We had shown 11 times. He had finished first five times, second four times, third once. Only once had he failed to finish in the ribbons. It was our one bad day, a 192.5. Was this dog on a roll or what?

■ CHAPTER 14 ■

Bionic Bebop

Bebop had finished his CDX in November of 1998. It would take many months to get him ready for the Utility ring.

We began immediately. Then, when Honeybear ruptured her anterior cruciate ligament early in 1999, I found myself with the opportunity, albeit unwanted, to focus exclusively on Bebop.

Disquieting things had begun to happen several years earlier. None was more telling than the trauma that took place as I introduced Bebop to go-outs, the first part of the directed jumping exercise.

Go-outs are difficult for the dog to understand. There are several ways to teach them, but the objective is the same no matter how you do it. The dog is supposed to run away from you on command. He must go straight as an arrow, heading for the midpoint of the other end of the ring — a pole that holds up rope or chain, or a center stanchion supporting baby gates, sometimes no pole or stanchion at all. He's supposed to keep going (theoretically to infinity) until you tell him to turn and sit, about 30 feet from you. But he must not turn, must not stop until you tell him to.

Debby likes to teach go-outs by putting a white pole in the ground, sending the dog and having him go around the pole. Knowing that he must go around the pole helps assure that he won't get in the habit of stopping short.

OK, that's how I'd teach Bebop.

Everything in obedience is taught in tiny increments. Everything! So I started close to the pole, within two or three feet. "Around!" I'd say, and I'd lure him around the pole with a treat, which he'd get as he completed the 180-degree turn.

Fine. It didn't take him long to understand that. The next step was to eliminate the lure, back up a few feet, send him, have him go around, then present his treat as a reward. That's when the uproar began. I'd send him from five feet out. He'd go to the pole. He knew where he was supposed to go. And that's where he stopped.

So I took him gently by the collar with the intent to guide him around the pole. And he *screeched*. It was as if I was branding him with a red-hot poker. I tried again. I made him go around, screeching all the way, in some form of terrible psychological pain. Then he got his treat.

I did that several times. He screeched his way around the pole several times. I found that I could send him on go-outs from ever-increasing distances and he'd go directly to the pole. But to force him to go around the pole was to jam a red-hot poker directly into his psyche. The pain must have been excruciating.

I told Debby about the problem. "You've got to push him through it, Willard," she said. Generally that was sound advice. In obedience competition training there are situations where you have to push the dog through, force him beyond the psychological obstacle (his or yours) in order to break through and get to the next level … an essential level.

As a Novice A trainer, I had resisted that with Honeybear. *I'll break her,* I thought. Or worse, *She won't love me.* In retrospect, I see the error of my ways.

So I persisted for two more days. I set up my white pole on the large grassy polo field at Paradise Valley Park. I'd send Bebop on a go-out. Happily he'd charge out there. But when I tried to make him circle that pole, he was upset beyond description.

At the end of the third day I told Debby, "That's it. There's no way I'll continue to upset my dog this badly. He goes out to the pole beautifully, and that'll be the end of it."

Indeed, as his career progressed, Bebop did beautiful go-outs. He'd charge out, arrow-straight, then turn and sit on a dime.

As all dogs will do, from time to time he lapsed into anticipating the turn and sit. ("Oh, I know what to do here. This is where I turn and sit. See how smart I am?") Then I'd go to him, take him by the collar and gently march him out to the post, the stanchion, whatever. And he'd cry, he'd shriek.

It took me awhile — many months, actually — to understand the syndrome. Bebop was obsessed with being right. Driven to be perfect. To learn that he had made a mistake, been *wrong*, killed his soul. And the first time he had protested being forced to go around the pole that obsession, that intensity, that drivenness had bubbled to the surface, never to submerge again.

Bebop never had to be corrected in the usual sense. Knowing he had made a mistake, knowing he was wrong, broke his heart. And while I had no inkling of it at the time, his searing anxiety about being wrong would, in the end, be his undoing.

Fortunately, he wasn't wrong very much. We spent many summer evenings training with Alice Blazer, the veterinarian who had done acupuncture on Honeybear as we tried to help HB's aging body hold up for those last few points needed for her OTCH. I'd set up a ring in the light from the tennis and basketball courts at Moon Valley Park. Bebop and I and Alice and Reba, her Australian shepherd, would go at it for a couple of hours. Countless times Alice shook her head and said, "I've never seen Bebop make a mistake." It was true. He was that good.

On the other hand, that depends on how you define "mistake." Several times during those sessions he crashed the high jump.

Summer here in Phoenix gets so blazing hot (112 degrees is not unusual) that it mandates training either at sunrise, about 5 A.M., or well after the sun goes down. Either time is just barely tolerable, and evening requires a light source.

We had a small Wednesday evening group at La Pradera Park, using the lights from the tennis courts. One summer evening during that session Bebop crashed the high jump so hard he knocked it over and dismantled the boards, even though they were bolted together. He was unharmed, not even rattled.

He had always been a wild jumper. A flat jumper. A kamikaze jumper. Sometimes he'd get so wound up over the exercise he'd take off 10 feet in front of the jump. Those watching at ringside would gasp. But Bebop was such a superb athlete, so abundantly muscled, that most of the time he could power himself right through his mistakes.

Most of the time, but not all the time. So when he crashed a jump we'd say, "There he goes again. Bebop, you're going to kill yourself." While my little lunatic was still a puppy, Debby had joked, "He's going to kill himself before he's five years old." From time to time across the years, I put him through a series of jumping programs to help him develop a better jumping style. To no avail.

■ ■ ■

After a bummer of a year with surgery, extensive rehabilitation and recovery, Honeybear came storming back to finish her OTCH on October 17, 1999. I was in seventh heaven. My Novice A dog was an Obedience Trial Champion.

Now I could focus on Bebop. Not that he had been neglected. Honeybear's months on the shelf had placed Bebop in number-one position for training. And he was ready.

He came out in Utility A on the last day of October. His Utility A career was short, one weekend. Honeybear had seen to that. Once a handler has put an OTCH on a dog, he may never again show in an A class at any level. The rest of his career will be spent in the B classes. Because I had already entered Bebop in Utility A before Honeybear finished her OTCH, we were permitted to show in the A class that weekend.

Bebop scored a 184 and took second place his first time out. Not much of a score, but Utility is tough for a green dog. Anytime you qualify on the way to your Utility Dog (UD) title, you beam from ear to ear and say, "I'll take it." And the fact that 184 was good for second place tells you a lot about the Utility A class. The day Honeybear got her first UD leg with 189 and a blue ribbon there were 13 dogs entered and she was the only one who qualified.

After that first and only Utility A weekend, we moved on to Utility B, where the judges' pencils would be a bit "sharper," and Bebop would get to go head to head with dogs who already had their OTCHs. "Now you'll be in there with the big dogs," I told him. *B classes, schmee classes,* he seemed to be saying as he finished his UD in four shows. His qualifying scores averaged exactly what he had scored in his first Utility class, 184.

Which foreshadowed the pattern for the rest of his career. He would never again be a high-scoring dog; his glory days had ended when he finished his CDX. On the other hand, it would be rare indeed when he failed to qualify. Bebop, the Great Entertainer, would be steady in a tornadic sort of way.

He finished his 1999 competition the weekend after Thanksgiving. The good news was he had gotten his UD. The bad news was he had shown only seven times in a year. Not exactly what I had had in mind for my rising star.

OK, he'd start his OTCH run at the Palm Springs shows early in January, and from there we'd pour it on.

■ ■ ■

Late in 1999 I noticed that Bebop was swiveling as he jumped. Torquing his hips in such a way as to shift the weight away from his right hip as he mostly pushed off with his left hind leg. That caught our attention. We immediately flashed back to that OFA X-ray in the summer of 1996 — the shallow socket and the malformed ball in the right hip.

That fall we spent Wednesday evenings at Phoenix Field and Obedience Club, doing ring procedures in a busy environment where 100 or so dogs were being trained. The ring run-throughs were conducted by Bea Dunn, a 40-year veteran in local dog obedience competition circles. After Bebop had finished his Utility run, Bea said, "Bebop's jumping funny." Indeed, he was swiveling again.

A week later, in the Open ring, I threw the dumbbell over the high jump, then sent Bebop to retrieve it. He hit the jump so hard he broke the top board, a two-inch by one-inch piece of wood. It fell to the ground in two pieces. Bebop recovered, snatched the dumbbell, returned over the remaining 20 inches of the jump and gave me a perfect front (albeit mouthing the dumbbell like a dog possessed).

My little guy has always lived a charmed life. Once, chasing a ball at dusk, he hit a rebar ring pole at full speed. The rebar bent to about 45 degrees. Bebop bounced off unhurt and retrieved the ball. Likewise, every one of his jump-crashing experiences left him uninjured and undaunted.

Nevertheless, enough was enough. I figured it was time to have Dr. Jim Boulay examine him. Dr. Boulay was the eminent Tucson veterinary surgeon who had done the highly successful tibial plateau-leveling osteotomy (TPLO) to repair Honeybear's torn anterior cruciate ligament ten months earlier.

Dr. Boulay's radiographs confirmed dysplasia in Bebop's right hip. And Bebop expressed pain in that hip when it was manipulated.

Dr. Boulay told me about a new type of artificial hip that was presently in clinical trials. It had been developed at the

University of Zurich and was called the Zurich Cementless Total Hip. The results had been good, he said. Among his own successful installations of the new hip was an Australian shepherd from New Mexico. The dog was again working sheep at full performance.

However, he suggested we proceed conservatively. "Let's try Rimadyl (a non-steroidal anti-inflammatory) for a while," he suggested. "Let's see if that helps him."

December passed without another jumping incident. Although I did see him transferring his weight several times.

Early in the afternoon of New Years Day I took both dogs to Moon Valley Park to practice. Barbara went along to help. This time she was there to see it happen. During the directed jumping exercise, Bebop crashed the jump so hard he turned it over. Fortunately it was my light practice jump and once more he emerged from the experience unhurt.

Barbara agreed that the accident happened because he couldn't generate enough thrust from his hind legs to propel him over the jump.

Later that afternoon I sent Dr. Boulay a fax. It began, "OK, I've had it."

Bebop received the Zurich Cementless Total Hip on January 12, 2000. Less than 24 hours later he walked out of the Southwest Veterinary Specialty Clinic on all four legs, not even limping. He stopped at the bushes near the door of the clinic, lifted his right hind leg and peed.

Barbara had gone with me to pick him up; we weren't sure what to expect. She sat in the back seat with him and he stood, leaning against her to steady himself, all the way back to Phoenix, 125 miles.

At the time of the OFA X-ray, I hadn't called Jennifer Howell. She was in Mississippi, we were in Arizona. The situation was what it was. She couldn't do a thing about it, and I didn't want to get embroiled in who did what to whom. I had training and showing to do; it was time to move on.

Now, though, I had closure on the saga of Bebop's right hip, so I decided it was time to update her. I told her about the OFA results. I told her about the titanium hip Bebop was now sporting. Then I told her about Dodie Green's revelations concerning Nick's alleged OFA excellent.

At that point Jennifer exploded in tears and rage. "Damn Bill Berhow! Damn him! He lied to me! And he's lied to lots of other people. He's been going around the country breeding that dog and telling everybody he's OFA excellent."

For the record, as I began work on this book, I checked my facts. On September 19, 2005, I called the Orthopedic Foundation for Animals to see for myself whether Nick had ever been OFA'd. "ABCA 1778 (that's Nick) does not show up in our records," they told me.

On the 21st of February we began a two-day trip to Denver. Alameda East Veterinary Hospital, famous as the setting for "Emergency Vet" on Animal Planet, was our destination. Robert Taylor, D.V.M., Alameda East's founder, had written the definitive texts on rehab for veterinary surgery patients.

Three days later Dr. Taylor and his staff met with us and put together a rehab plan for my little guy.

Let's see, a year earlier I had been nursing Honeybear, following her TPLO. Now it was Bebop with a new hip. I wondered if we should be showing in the Utility ring or at veterinary grand rounds.

■ ■ ■

Things got worse. Late in April Ron Sigler, D.V.M., the senior veterinary ophthalmologist in our area, removed rapidly growing cataracts from both of Bebop's eyes and inserted intraocular lenses.

The next four weeks were hairy. Anything that results in an impact on the eyes following that type of veterinary surgical procedure can be disastrous. Major damage may result. In short, allow the dog to jump, run, fall, carry on at the front door, roughhouse with the other dogs, or race out the back door joyously barking at and chasing birds, and you are likely to blow the whole thing.

The objective was to keep Bebop absolutely quiet for a month. Hearing that, those who knew border collies responded with some version of, "Yeah, right." And those who knew my little maniac personally laughed out loud. What they didn't understand was, we have, "I'm going to keep him quiet." And then we have, "*By God* I'm going to keep him quiet." I had determined it would be the latter.

"Just keep him in a crate for a month," some ventured. And have him ricochet off the sides of the crate when someone comes to the door?

No! We went into battened-down mode.

For the next four weeks, Barbara and I coordinated our schedules so that one of us would be home at all times. All three dogs were sequestered in whatever room we were in, under constant surveillance. We added breadth and depth to the cliché 24/7.

The front of the house, particularly the front door, was our Achilles heel. All blinds with exposure to the street were drawn and closed. The doorbell was disconnected. We headed off doorpounders by stretching yellow crime scene tape at several levels between the light posts on either side of our front walk. A large wicker basket was placed in front of the tape. A sign said, *Do Not Go Beyond This Point. Put Deliveries In The Basket.* God help anyone who violated that barricade.

No one did. No UPS delivery man came sprinting up the walk. No Seventh Day Adventists strolled slowly to our door.

And the procession of illegal immigrants wanting to trim our palms was temporarily halted.

And how did "Bionic Bebop" emerge from all this? When he was fully recovered, he jumped like a deer and saw like a hawk.

■ CHAPTER 15 ■

Metamorphosis

Before I knew it, most of 2000 had slipped by. My little guy was preparing to get in there with the "big dogs" ... again. He had shown only 10 times in 42 months. He may have been 6½ years old, but he was still a green obedience competition dog.

Along the way a strange metamorphosis had taken place. Bebop had always been gung-ho. I liked to tell people my little guy was 48 pounds of want-to. *Driven* was probably a more appropriate word. But wasn't that why I had gotten a border collie? Wasn't gung-honess the quality that had first attracted me to Ott?

My border collie was wild and crazy, shot from a gun. And I loved every minute of it. He was also fast, accurate and obsessively focused on me. I loved that, too.

When Bebop was in Novice, his heeling was superb. After all, it was perfect scores in both on-leash and off-leash heeling that had contributed to that near-perfect score the second time he walked into a Novice B ring. By the time we showed in Open, he had begun to inch forward during heeling, but he got out front and held that position. A local judge, the late Bob Little, told me that many judges score border collies differently from the way they score other dogs. "They expect a little forging from border collies," he said. "It's a border collie thing. If the dog gets out there and holds his position, the judge will regard that as his normal heeling position and won't score it."

I found that to be true. In capturing our three Open A blue ribbons, we posted scores of 197, 195 and 195½. A point or a point and a half was about what the judges saw during our heel-free and figure eight. Where they crucified us was in response to Bebop's frantic chomping on the dumbbell as he brought it back to me. "Frantic" means that by the time he got to front he was chomping so hard that with each bite his head shot forward and the dumbbell banged against my knee.

He was also getting more vocal.

In the Open classes, the group sits and downs are three and five minutes, respectively, with handlers out of sight. In his entire career Bebop did not break a sit or a down in competition.

But while he may have looked like a statue during the group exercises, he sure didn't sound like one. About the time he graduated to the Open classes he began whining during the out-of-sight sits and downs. On one or two occasions early in his Open career I returned to the ring during the group exercises to have the judge tell me, "Your dog was whining while you were gone." I knew it was true because as I had walked away from him to leave the ring, I had heard soft crying noises behind me, and I knew it was my dog. Those little episodes would cost us one or two points to spoil what would otherwise be perfect group exercises.

It was happening during the group exercises in class as well, and Debby suggested a strategy to resolve the problem.

Why was Bebop whining? Because he was uncomfortable sitting out there in that line of dogs while I left him and disappeared for a few minutes. If we could make him more comfortable, he might stop whining. So the goal was to make the group exercises a pleasant experience. A short period of time where he'd focus on the expectation that something good might happen rather than dwelling on his plight.

During the Open group exercises, while the handlers were required to leave the ring, the judge and one or two stewards would remain. "When we do the group exercises in class and in practice matches, we'll have the judge, a steward, anyone who is staying in the ring, periodically walk over and give Bebop a treat," Debby suggested. "He'll soon come to think of the group exercises as a really neat place to be."

"Right on," I said.

The next opportunity came at a practice match. Debby instructed the judge. The long sit was first. Before I got out of the ring, the judge walked over to Bebop, said, "Good sit," and gave my surprised border collie a treat. Then, at intervals of about a minute, she gave him two more goodies.

"Did he whine?" I asked as I returned to the ring. "Not at all," the judge replied. "Now he won't take his eyes off of me."

We repeated the game during the long down. The result was the same. Feeding Bebop during sits and downs was not a transient ploy. It became a fixture in his obedience training, one that lasted for as long as he showed in competition.

It certainly shifted his thoughts away from his anxieties. We'd walk into the ring for the group exercises, whether it be practice or the real thing, and Bebop would lock onto the judge. I couldn't even get him to glance at me, which in that setting didn't matter.

Pretty soon others became aware of our little game and saw that it was working. Before long, in any line of dogs, a handful were being fed while their handlers were out of sight.

At that time I was taking Bebop to ring run-throughs at PFOC one night a week. Harry Burke was conducting the run-throughs. Harry is a local judge who has volunteered in many roles for PFOC across more than two decades.

One night during sits and downs, Harry had ten dogs in the line. Seven of them were getting treats, which kept Harry busy. When the exercises were over, Harry laughed and told the group, "The next time I judge anywhere around here half the dogs in the ring won't stop staring at me."

The group exercises weren't the only place where Bebop was giving vent to his burgeoning anxieties. The shrieking incident that had stunned me when I tried to get him to go around the go-out pole proved to be a preview of things to come.

Bebop made darn few mistakes in practice; Alice Blazer could attest to that. But when he did he had to be told that what he had just done was wrong, then shown what was right. More and more that set him off.

Understand that when he screwed up he was not "corrected" in the classic negative sense too often associated with dog obedience training. He was never jerked around by the collar. He was never even ear-pinched. Lack of motivation was never an issue with Bebop. Excess motivation definitely was. From the day I carried him into the house, the little guy redefined the words *work ethic*. He was obsessed with doing his "job" and doing it right.

If I threw the dumbbell and it went under the ring gate and came to rest six inches on the other side, somebody better hustle out there and bring it back before Bebop tore out there and demolished that end of the ring so he could retrieve it. The night he crashed the jump and shattered the top board I doubt he even knew it; he was hellbent to retrieve that dumbbell and bring it to me. That was his *job* for God's sake.

When Bebop made a mistake, my first responsibility was to let him know what he had done wrong. That flies in the face of how many people train. The dog makes a mistake and they simply have him repeat the behavior or the exercise. They're so focused on teaching the dog what's right that he never understands what's wrong, never learns to discriminate between right and wrong.

If Bebop cut short a go-out, I'd take him by the collar and lead him out to where he was supposed to have gone. He'd shriek all the way. If he anticipated, I'd put him back where he should have waited. And I'd hear about it.

It was the moment of finding out he was wrong that broke his heart. He was never aggressive about it, never nasty, just crushed.

■ CHAPTER 16 ■

Too Smart?

One of the reasons I had wanted a border collie was because everywhere I turned it seemed someone was raving, "Border collies! Oh, they're so smart!" And watching Ott once or twice a week left no doubt: Yeah, they were smart all right.

Bebop did not disappoint. He was incredibly smart. He understood what everything was about. So it didn't take him long to figure out that obedience trials were THE SHOW! The place where it was all on the line. The one place in the world where he most wanted to get it right. So he tried even harder, ratcheted up his intensity level. Psyched himself to a fever pitch.

The judges loved him (love which did not necessarily flow down pencils and onto score sheets). Crowds gathered at ringside, fascinated. They clapped vigorously when we finished ... regardless of how well we had done. The whole scene was enhanced by the fact that Bebop was a big, strong, handsome guy. That was no junkyard cur cutting up in there.

Fellow competitors would ask, "When are you and Bebop in? I don't want to miss that." Then, after our run, "How do you get him up like that? I wish I could get my dog that motivated."

Of course, what I *wanted* to do was tone the whole thing down.

■ ■ ■

By the time Bebop got back into competition in the fall of 2000, every activity to which the adjective *hyper* could be applied had ascended to a new level of intensity.

They'd call us into the ring. Once inside I'd remove his leash and hand it to the steward. Immediately Bebop would start to spin, run around me in circles, occasionally jumping on my back. All the way to the starting point for the next exercise. Once there I'd say, "Place!" Instantly he'd be at my left side. But it would take two more tight spins before he'd settle into perfect heel position, head up, focused, saying, "Let's go!"

His obsession to be perfect was wound tighter, too. And it began costing us in the ring. Mostly on the heeling exercises. When we heeled, he was forged a third of a body length and wrapped around in front of me. I liked to tell people that he wanted to look into my eyes, both of them.

I'm slew-footed. It's a trait that runs in my family. When I walk, my left foot points some 30 or 40 degrees to the left. Debby was the first to point out that Bebop, whose wrapping put him directly in the path of that left foot, had mastered perfect timing, the synchronism of stepping over that foot as we heeled.

We returned to the ring at a three-day cluster in Las Vegas. On the second day we finished second in Open B and the Bopster picked up his first OTCH point. The next morning he won Utility B and got four more points. Despite all his hijinks, his forging, his wrapping, his anticipation, his voracious mouthing of the dumb-bell and scent articles, my little guy was on his way again.

Bebop's ring appearances were a strange blend of the brilliant and the ludicrous. Whenever speed was a factor in an exercise, or when he could make it a factor, he was breathtaking. On the go-outs he would go like a scalded dog, straight as an arrow. When I called, "Bebop, sit!" he would turn on a dime and plant.

He worked the scent articles at the speed of light. We were at the Orange Empire shows in San Bernardino, California. A representative from the Canadian Kennel Club (CKC) was there. Before competition started, she struck up a conversation with Barbara. "We are thinking of making some changes in our obedience regulations north of the border," she said, "and I'm here this weekend to observe." When Bebop and I went into the ring for our Utility B run, the CKC woman was standing next to Barbara. As Bebop went about his business at the scent articles pile, she gasped and said, "I've never seen a dog work articles that fast."

And guess what, Bebop was not only lightning fast. In a household of excellent scent articles dogs, he holds the record: 340 correct scent articles in a row in matches and shows.[2] He was a machine. Of course, I went through several sets of scent articles each year because when he returned with the article, he was chomping on it with gusto.

He'd retrieve a dumbbell at warp speed, then return to a perfect front and mouth it so violently that he was banging out a tattoo on my knees. Someone said, "Willard, you better wear a cup when you work that dog." Fortunately I'm tall enough that knee pads would have been more appropriate.

Once I learned of a guy in the Midwest who custom-made really nice dumbbells. So I did all the proper measuring and ordered one. Unfortunately he had used a soft wood. The dumbbell came. We went out to train. Bebop had retrieved it no more than half a dozen times when there I stood with part of the new dumbbell in my right hand, the other part in my left. He had chomped right through it.

---

[2] As OTCH Dreams was going to press, Cheddar, my golden retriever, set a new household record, 509 in a row.

In the Utility ring, we were a cinch to lose about three points per run as a result of his mouthing: a point on each scent article, one more on the glove.

Our total score in each ring hinged on how a particular judge regarded Bebop's "heel position." Bob Little had been right. Some judges seemed to expect a border collie to be out front and *slightly* wrapped — so long as he didn't oscillate, up and back, up and back. Others, well, as soon as Bebop moved forward, they'd go into a writing frenzy, adding up numbers . faster than the pump at a California gas station.

The difference in judges' perception hit home one morning in Las Vegas. First, in Open B, under "Judge A," we lost nine points on the heel-free and figure eight. Less than two hours later, under "Judge B," Bebop's heeling wasn't one bit different. Yet we lost only two points on the signal exercise (heeling and hand signals). Go figure.

Another time in Open B, my little maniac decided to feature the mother of all wraps at the very instant the judge called a fast. That could have spelled disaster. But I leaped over him, he quickly slid back into heel position and we lost *one* point on the exercise.

Action approaching that extreme was not unusual when Bebop and I heeled. It was a circus. Or a rodeo? Once, after a particularly wild "ride," Debby was standing outside the ring, laughing as we emerged. "Ride 'em, cowboy!" she yelled. "You hung on to the eight-second buzzer."

Often, at obedience trials, particularly in California, we'd run into Joe and Janet Devine. Joe had wonderful golden retrievers, OTCH dogs. Janet had a border collie, Trinket. Like Bebop, Trinket was capable of brilliant performances or weekend-wrecking disasters in the ring. Trinket wasn't but could have been a littermate of Bebop, at least as far as heeling was concerned: shot from a gun, out front, wrapped.

Janet and I settled into having little fun contests. Whichever dog lost the most points on a heeling exercise was the winner for that day.

"OK, Trinket lost six points on the heel-free and figure eight."

"Too bad, Bebop lost seven. We win."

Despite our lighthearted kidding and the crowd appreciation Bebop's performances elicited, I was concerned. He almost always held it together well enough to qualify, but our scores were more often in the high 180s than the low to mid-190s. He was piling up UDX legs at a steady rate, but with the kinds of scores he was getting, OTCH points were hard to come by. And Super Dog? We were a far cry from working at that level.

■ ■ ■

Kay Guetzloff was realistic about our situation. At the time, she and Dick were still living in Arizona. While Dick traveled a lot in his quest to set what was then the all-time OTCH points record, Kay was often at ringside when Bebop and I showed locally.

One day she analyzed our last few Utility scores. She took them exercise by exercise and highlighted where we regularly lost points. When she finished, she told me, "In order to be really competitive, you need to add about eight points to your average score." She shook her head. "That's next to impossible in a dog this age (seven) who's been showing this long. If we were talking two points, maybe. But ..."

That same morning we talked at length about Bebop's demeanor in the competition ring: his spinning, his jumping up my back, his general wildness. Of course I already knew there were plenty of border collies like Bebop; it wasn't an aberration, it just presented control headaches.

"In my experience," Kay told me — and she had more than 30 years of it — "border collies with that sort of temperament only get worse as they get older." In my lifetime, no one has ever told me anything that turned out to be more profound.

■ ■ ■

Mouthing was Bebop's second biggest problem. Second only because the heeling transgressions presented a much larger window of opportunity for the judge to deduct points. When my little guy returned to front with a dumbbell or a glove or a scent article, he had only a few seconds to wreak havoc before the judge mercifully said, "Take it." At which point I would summon up Medal of Honor courage, reach into the area of those snapping fangs and remove the dumbbell. Which, by the way, Bebop, dying to please, always gave up readily.

I tried all the standard ways to eliminate his mouthing. Simply placing it behind his canines, then gently clamping his mouth

Photo: Bill Kohler & Associates

Bebop's UDX, April 2001

shut, one hand atop his nose, the other beneath his jaw. Tugging with the dumbbell to encourage him to clamp down and stay clamped down until I told him to release it. Having him heel with the dumbbell in his mouth; this to give him something else to think about while he held the dumbbell.

All these remedial attempts worked well in isolation but had little effect on his chomping during the exercises we were trying to clean up.

We tried a few offbeat things as well. One that was more fun than effective was the biscuit trick. First I taught him to balance a dog biscuit on top of his nose and hold it there until I said, "OK!" At which point he'd flip it off his nose and, after a fair amount of practice, catch it in midair.

The next step was to place the dumbbell in his mouth and the biscuit on his nose. If he chomped, the biscuit fell off and he'd be ... *wrong!* After a few seconds (which increased incrementally), I'd say, "Out," carefully remove the dumbbell so as not to disturb the biscuit, followed a few seconds later by "OK!"

Bebop got quite skilled at walking around with the dumbbell clamped solidly between his teeth and the biscuit balanced precariously on his nose. As usual, he was intensely focused. His eyes were crossed as he tried to watch the biscuit as we went.

Eventually, the day before a trial, we were setting up our tent. Dick Guetzloff was there. "Let me show you something, Dick," I said. And Bebop and I performed: dumbbell in mouth, biscuit on nose.

Dick smiled. "That's very cute," he said, "but when the biscuit goes away, he's going to mouth."

As usual, Dick was right. And several of the superstars of the sport of dog obedience told me flat out, "You're never going to eliminate that." They, too, were right. Ultimately I settled for trying to keep it down to a dull roar and taking our lumps in the ring.

The forging/wrapping problem was another matter entirely. As Bebop's career progressed, so did his desire to please. Which translated into him inching farther and farther forward and wrapping more and more. Judges were killing us on the heeling exercises. When he wrapped so badly that I was in imminent danger of pitching over him and going flat on my face, even the most lenient judges were going to crucify us.

■ CHAPTER 17 ■

Pinpoint Heeling

Louise Meredith first showed up on my radar screen in 1995. Gaines fever was still rampaging through my body and my mind. At shows it was all about Honeybear. But Bebop was a year old and I was alert to anything and everything that would help me cope with this oh-so-different kind of dog. Wherever we went to show, I watched the border collies and lapped it up.

We'd arrive at the show site the afternoon before the trial and set up our tent. When we were showing in Southern California, Louise would be there, too, setting up and working her border collies. She had this stick thing that protruded from her armband. She'd put a soft treat on it and heel her dog around the setup area. The dog would be in perfect heel position, head up, focused on that impaled treat. I was fascinated.

More often than not, the following two days would feature Louise and her dog — Lace at that time — stepping forward to accept blue ribbons, high-in-trial trophies, high-combined awards.

Honeybear and I were in Pasadena in mid-December of 1996, competing in the Los Encinos Kennel Club obedience trial at Brookside Park. We qualified in both B classes that day to pick up our seventh UDX leg. That put us in the Open B ring when Judge Keith Coyne handed out the awards. After he was finished, he asked those present to linger a bit longer for something special. Then he announced that Louise Meredith was retiring Lace (OTCH Highland's Chantilly Lace UDX) that day with 1062 OTCH points.

That blew me away. By that time, HB and I had struggled to accumulate nine points. Back home in Phoenix, I said to Barbara, "Remember that woman who heels her dog around with that stick thing on her arm? She just retired her dog with 1062 OTCH points. Wow!"

Thereafter, Louise and whatever border collie she was showing at the time became to Bebop and me what Karen Price and Flash had been to Honeybear and me when we were starting out — our role models.

In March of 1997, Honeybear and I got it all together and beat Louise and her great border collie Riot in a runoff for high in trial at the Palm Springs Kennel Club show. It was a special, special day.

Mostly I admired Louise and her border collies from a distance, venturing timid "Good mornings" at shows. Ultimately, though, with Bebop's heeling a disaster, I broke through and asked her for advice.

The first thing Louise ever said to me was one of those timeless gems. I had asked her, "How do you keep your border collies from forging?"

Her reply was, "I don't ever let them get started." Now older, wiser and with many more scars on my psyche, I appreciate the wisdom of that declaration. You don't have to incur a cerebral hernia trying to "fix" something that has never gotten a foothold.

Back when I was starting Honeybear and wondering which end of the leash you attach to the dog, the big hotshot in obedience was Bernie Brown. His dog, OTCH Tanbark's Bristol Creme UDX, had been named Kennel Ration Dog of the Year multiple times, and at the time had amassed more OTCH points than any dog in history, 5,621. Bristol was a golden retriever, which caught my attention big time.

Bernie taught a heeling method that was unique. When practicing heeling, he tethered his young dog to his left leg in perfect heel position. This went on for many months, until the dog was conditioned that perfect heel position was the only place to be.

So Louise's advice that the dog never be allowed to develop bad heeling habits was not new.

I had seen Louise practicing heeling with her dogs, using that stick on her armband with the soft treat serving as a focal point. I understood that the stick with the treat were essentials in keeping the dog in perfect heel position. But that's about all I understood. So I found out where to get the "attention stick," the stick-holder and armband, ordered them and began to use them the day they arrived.

What I didn't know was that when I saw Louise heeling her dog around in perfect position, focused on that armband treat, I was seeing the final step in a process. A process that evolved out of the teachings of AnneMarie Silverton, in my opinion the most astute competition obedience instructor of our time.

As I would later learn, ideally the process begins when the OTCH-aspiring dog is still a tiny puppy, maybe seven weeks old.

■ ■ ■

Assuming the person teaching this method is *you*, here we go.

The method doesn't even begin with heel position. It starts with your puppy in front of you. You begin by slowly walking backwards, holding a piece of food in your hand, presenting it for your puppy to nibble. All the while saying, "Strut!"

Pretty soon the puppy knows the treat is there and you can hold it a few inches from his nose. As soon as he's focused on the food, has all four feet on the floor and is giving you a cute little strut, say, "Get it!" It's a good idea to have him jump slightly to get his treat. That builds enthusiasm, drive.

Soon these little follow games progress to wide circles, zig-zag patterns, passes between and around your legs, etc. Your puppy loves these exercises, and they are helping him become more agile.

Before long you can start to hold the treat in your left hand — conspicuously between your thumb and index finger — and begin to coax Flea into heel position.

At first you continue to hold the food close to your little guy's nose, allowing him to nibble, in order to hold his attention and keep his head up. Then gradually — very gradually — you begin to raise the treat; his head should follow it. If it doesn't, lower the food enough to recapture his full attention — all the way to the nibble point, if necessary. At this point it's likely to be a prolonged game of raising the food, lowering the food, raising the food to keep his attention. Eventually he's heeling (after a fashion) with his head up and his eyes locked on the treat, which has ascended to waist level.

There is a pitfall lurking here, an important one. The objective is to teach Flea to maintain perfect heel position. The treat in the hand is a tool to create a focal point, one that marks perfect heel position. If the hand with the food wanders around, the perfectly positioned focal point is lost.

You must find a way to anchor that target hand so the treat and your dog's attention stay precisely where you want them. That's not easy to do; you have plenty of other things to think about as you attempt your first little baby steps of heeling with your puppy. When possible, it helps to have a training buddy watch you and tell you if your arm is moving. In any case, *hold your arm still* or you'll blow the whole thing.

There's a corollary pitfall here: taking the treat to the dog rather than insisting that the dog come to the treat. In your anxiousness to have Flea in the right position — that space between his eyes centered directly under the food is ideal — you may tend to move the food to make it happen.

Don't! Again, you'll blow the whole thing.

When you are at this stage, you are doing mostly straight-line heeling and large circles to the left and right. After you have good attention on these basic patterns, you can begin to introduce informal left turns (at this point they don't have to be precise), right turns, about turns, slows and fasts.

The cue words remain the same: "Strut!" to make him focus on the treat, "Get it!" to make him jump up for the food. Jumping to get his treat is an additional reminder to keep his head up.

It's important at this point to do only tiny increments of heeling — two or three steps of just what you want: head up, little guy in perfect heel position. The oh-so-easy-to-make mistake here is stretching your luck. Flea's head is up. He's right where you want him. You feel your oats. "Ooh, let's go a few steps more." Which you do. And just as you draw in your breath to say, "Get it!" Flea drops his head or lags or forges. And that's what gets rewarded.

At this point we settle in to letting the behavior get solidly reinforced. Flea's thinking, *I stay right here next to Mom's pants seam, I keep my head up nice and high … and shazam! I get a goody.*

When that's solid, when you've summoned up the self-control to reinforce what you want in tiny, easy-to-manage steps, it's time to move on.

Next we introduce a small stick that we call the *attention stick.* It's about one-eighth inch in diameter and about seven inches long. Ideally you should hold the stick in your right hand, across your body, at about waist level. That frees your left hand to hold a leash or foil your dog's treat-stealing efforts.

However, if you have short arms or abundant avoirdupois, you may be unable to reach all the way across your body. In that case, hold the stick in your left hand. Either way, find a way to anchor the stick so it doesn't wander.

At all points in this process, Flea is going to try to steal the food. That's good: he sees it, he's interested in it, he wants it. He's primed to learn to focus on it. If he doesn't try to steal it, you'd better get busy and find something that does motivate him.

While his interest in stealing the food is a positive sign, that doesn't mean you should allow it. And the fact that you shouldn't allow it doesn't mean you'll always be able to prevent it. But you should try. In the early stages, when the treat is still in your hand, a firm "Leave it!" as you pull your hand away will suffice.

Later, when the treat's on the stick and the stick is in your right hand, your left hand will be free to fend off your pillaging dog. While it is important to condition Flea that he doesn't get his treat until you say, "Get it!" the problem should eradicate itself later in the process.

Now that you have the food on the stick, it is more visible to your dog than it was between your thumb and forefinger. It's sitting out there on the end of the stick, all by itself. AnneMarie Silverton, who developed this method, calls it "pinpoint heeling." And it's at this point — with the food sitting out there as a focus beacon, and with skillful handling of the attention stick — that precision can be achieved.

That is, *if* the stick is properly positioned. It's important to hold that stick so it's constantly even with the seam of your pants. Handlers have a tendency to allow the hand, hence the stick, to drift forward, causing the dog at least to forge, maybe to wrap. Find a way to anchor that stick hand. Note, however, that you're still free to move the stick up and down to hold Flea's attention.

At this point Flea's head should be up and looking at the stick ... consistently. What if it isn't? First, be certain that he *understands* what you expect — head up, looking at the treat on the stick. Once you're sure he understands, if he chooses not to comply, then a correction is necessary. Simply pop up on the leash, point to the food and say, "Strut!" Then, when he's in correct position, "Get it!" And terminate the exercise.

Get Flea comfortable with the stick, the food, the position. Demand perfection! Demand less and Flea will give you less.

Don't rush to the next step, but eventually it will be time for an equipment change. We use a belt with a plate that has a small threaded hole to accommodate the stick. When Flea is a "seasoned veteran" with the hand-held stick, the stick screws into the plate. Now you have the belt around your waist, the plate adjusted to sit centered above your pants seam, the stick screwed into the plate, and the food on the end of the stick.

This arrangement leaves both hands free of encumbrances, and you're liberated from the problem of the drifting stick; it's anchored right where you want it.

All things in obedience training progress in small increments. Which means you're going to hold the progression at this point until Flea is doing really well. What does "really well" mean? It means your dog's focus should not stray from the focal point you have created with that tasty goody parked out there on the end of the stick. And his position should not deviate from exactly where you want him. At this point in teaching your dog to heel, the time for *almost, close to, in the general vicinity of* is long since past.

Can you heel him down the center aisle at PetSmart with nary a flicker in his attention? How about outside The Home Depot, right where the contractors bang around as they pick up

Photo: Unknown

Louise and National Obedience Champion Twister

their materials? Can you navigate a line of hot dog slices with unbroken attention? And what if someone walks alongside and touches Flea?

If your answer to the above questions is "Gangbusters!" maybe, just maybe, you're ready for the *piece de resistance* of this process: the armband's armband.

Now we realize what this is all about. What are you allowed to take into the ring with you that will help your dog maintain heel position? Certainly not treats. Not a toy. What then? Your armband! And the armband is always in the place that represents perfect heel position. Which means if you can teach Flea to focus on your armband he should be in heel position.

To accomplish this, we now bring into play one more piece of specialized equipment, a Velcroed armband that goes around your bicep, fitting over your regulation armband. The Velcroed armband also has a small plate into which a treat-impaling stick can be screwed.

At this point the dog is unlikely to try to steal the treat. Now it's much easier to pick just the right moment, say, "Get it!" and have Flea jump for the reward. (Some handlers who have small dogs wear a wristband instead of the armband.) At appropriate moments, the handler should point to the food on the armband stick and say, "Strut!" in order to refocus the dog's attention. AnneMarie and the California proponents of the pinpoint heeling method use "Strut!" as their command to get the dog moving with head up. Then "Strut!" again to remind Flea where his eyes and his attention should be focused.

At the point where the stick moves up to armband height, it can protrude several inches. Then, in tiny increments, you can cut it back until it's hardly more than a nub, just enough to hold a soft treat.

Later, much later, when Flea is just about ready to explode upon the world of AKC obedience competition, you should turn the Velcroed armband around so that the stick/nub is under your arm. Now you can conceal the treat or its absence. As you practice, sometimes the food will be there, sometimes it won't. But in Flea's mind, *it could be.*

It may take the dog a few tries to figure out the new location of his treat. The method remains the same: "Get it!" Lift your arm. Flea jumps and grabs his goody.

The special armband can be used right up until seconds before you are called into the ring. Just remember to take it off before you enter the ring.

■ ■ ■

The section you have just completed offered a detailed explanation of what I *didn't* understand when I started using the stick on the armband in an attempt to pull Bebop back into heel position. I had seen this woman with these great border collies. And she was forever heeling them around with this stick on her armband. It worked for her, why shouldn't it work for me?

Because I hadn't built the foundation, that's why. I put the armband on, stuck food on it and Bebop went merrily on his way, a foot in front of my alleged focal point, and wrapped dangerously around in front of my left leg.

Live and learn. Which I did much later ... with another dog. But that's another book.

■ ■ ■

Note: The pinpoint heeling equipment mentioned in this chapter — the stick, the belt, the armband, etc. — are available from Janet Devine. Her email address is:

Sewdevine1@sbcglobal.net

■ CHAPTER 18 ■

Such ... Such What?

Despite Bebop's wildness, his between-exercises shenanigans, his forging and wrapping, his anticipation, his preeminence as The Great Entertainer, we did surprisingly well. It became clear he would never be a high-scoring dog, never the Super Dog winner of my dreams. Not that Super Dog even mattered anymore. In the fall of 2000, The Gaines had its last hurrah. After 25½ years of thrilling, inspiring competitions, The Gaines went belly-up for lack of a major sponsor. Just about the time Bebop and I would have *been* there, fate intervened and spared us the embarrassment of *not* being there.

Nevertheless, my little guy and I were hard at it in our own little world, occasionally kicking butts and taking points. It was a rare day when the Bopster didn't qualify in both B rings. And occasionally we'd pick up an OTCI point or two. It was even more rare to make it through a weekend without at least one of our judges saying, "He's *so* excited," or "He doesn't love this *much*, does he?" or "Such enthusiasm!" or "Such energy!"

Thank God they saw it that way. They could just as well have drilled us with what is known in the sport as "points below the line." On the judge's scoresheet, there's a space labeled Penalty for Misbehavior. Any judge could have socked it to us, and I wouldn't have said one word of protest.

The thing was, Bebop radiated want-to, and he presented a package of speed, accuracy and animal magnetism that caused judges to chuckle rather than write.

As we lurched through 2000 and 2001, bouncing off walls that no one else could see, I kept hearing all those words: energy! enthusiasm! excitement! People would come up to me at ringside and ask, "How do you get your dog *up* like that? I wish I could get that kind of energy out of my dog."

I'd hear those comments and give some sort of wiseass answer: "I give him want-to pills." But more and more I heard a little voice inside my head saying, "Is that what I'm seeing, pure joy, over-the-top enthusiasm? Or is it something darker?"

Others — most notably Debby Boehm and Louise Meredith — were saying, "You've got to get him under control between exercises; your scores will get a lot better." I tried. In practice I began using an approach I called the "seamless exercise." From the moment we entered the ring or the area where we were going to practice, Bebop was under command. I heeled him from one exercise to the next, allowing no chance for his hijinks. It worked in practice.

And it fell apart when we got to the shows. As soon as we stepped into the ring, it was, "Let's party!" and the fun began.

Late in 2001 I decided to try another approach. Bebop obeyed my commands in the same manner in which he went about everything else: as if he were shot from a gun. From the time he was a young dog, if I would say, "Place!" (his command to get into heel position) he would come flying from across the room or the yard and swing into perfect position next to my left leg.

A couple of times I was working Honeybear and forgot Bebop was within earshot. I would tell HB, "Place!" and here would come this black streak out of nowhere. It was comical to see the two of them jockeying for perfect heel position. Bebop would not be denied. He would put his shoulder down and bull his way between Honeybear and my left leg. Such intensity! Such an obsession to be perfect!

So why not use that? The circus came to town between exercises. Why not simply eliminate that window of opportunity?

Late in 2001, in practice, I began finishing an exercise, pivoting in front of my little maniac and saying, "Stay!" (He was already sitting.) Then I'd walk to the point where the next exercise would begin, position myself and call, "Place!" Bebop would come flying across the ring and swing into heel position, ready to go. Mission accomplished.

There was disagreement about how that tactic would wash with AKC judges. Would they view it as training in the ring? I thought not. *I'm only calling my dog into position to start the next exercise,* I reasoned.

We have several AKC obedience judges living here in the Valley of the Sun. So I tested my ploy. They didn't agree. One said, "Oh, no! That's training in the ring." Another said, "I wouldn't object to that, you're just controlling your dog."

Harry Burke, a veteran judge, likes to tell handlers, "Never do anything in the ring that causes a judge to think." Sound advice.

What was required was to find out for myself, to test it in the real thing.

The next real thing would come the weekend after Thanksgiving at the shows put on by Sahuaro State Kennel Club. Sahuaro State is a club that across the years has never been able to find a home. Their shows have bounced all over the Valley. Honeybear and I first encountered them on our very own "home" field, the polo field at Paradise Valley Park. Later they would show indoors at Phoenix Convention Center. Then indoors at the Arizona State Fairgrounds. Followed by outdoors at the Fairgrounds.

In November of 2001 they landed in a quirky setting, a swap meet in the far Southwest Valley. It was a place that seemingly couldn't make up its mind whether it was indoors or outdoors. It was covered overhead and open on the sides, a wind tunnel as it turned out. The swap meet wasn't doing well and there was plenty of extra space … on the cheap. The club put down black rubber mats and set up ring gates. Parking was scarcely 100 feet away. All in all, not too bad … until it was time to show.

Saturday morning was cold and squally. The wind gusted through the trial area, bringing all sorts of interesting debris into the ring at all the wrong times.

The judges were Larry and Pauline Andrus, veterans and good. Our first ring was Open B, the domain of Pauline. The first exercise was the heel free and figure eight. At the conclusion of the figure eight I told Bebop, "Stay!" and walked across the ring to position myself for the drop on recall. Mrs. Andrus watched with interest. Then I said, "Bebop, place!" He flew across the ring and shot into heel position. For the first time in his competition career there were no shenanigans between exercises.

Mrs. Andrus gave the instructions. I walked to the other end of the ring. On my commands, Bebop came like a bullet and dropped like he had been shot. Nice job.

The retrieve on the flat would be done from the spot where the drop on recall had finished. As Mrs. Andrus approached to hand me the dumbbell, she said softly, "Before that last exercise it looked like you were training in the ring."

"I was just trying to control my dog between exercises," I replied.

"But it looked like training in the ring," she persisted.

"Are you saying I shouldn't do that?"

The judge nodded, "That's what I'm saying."

So much for that stroke of brilliance. It had seemed like a great idea, too.

■■■

In spite of Mrs. Andrus' caution about training in the ring, in spite of tripping over Bebop on an about turn and nearly going down in a heap, we scored a 191 in Open B. I was relieved. It could have been worse, I thought. I had shown in windy Las Vegas often enough to know that wind makes wild border collies wilder. And that morning at the outdoor-indoor trial, Bebop had ratcheted it up a few notches.

As his career had progressed, he had become more and more aware of not screwing up at the "Big Shows." As 2001 wound down, I could feel him trying harder, getting more and more intense. The words "fever pitch" now most aptly described his demeanor in the ring. Somewhere enthusiasm had segued into frenzy.

From time to time as we prepared to enter the ring, and once in a while between exercises, he would bleat in a manner that reminded me of that shrieking I first heard the day I tried to get him to go around the pole. Not as loud, but it had the same genesis.

That morning in Mrs. Andrus' ring he did it several times as we were setting up to begin an exercise. More often than ever before. I was afraid she might score us on it, but she seemed not to notice.

When we came out of the ring, someone said, "He was really wound up this morning."

Yes, he was.

■■■

I pulled Bebop from Utility B that morning. Larry Andrus' ring was in the teeth of the wind. Several times I saw a dog come over a jump only to be met with a mat blowing up in his face like a tsunami. With a dog who had a history of jumping problems, I sure didn't need that.

Following the Sahuaro State shows, we weren't scheduled to show again until the Phoenix Field and Obedience Club trials, the 23rd and 24th of February. A longer layoff than we'd had since Bebop's cataract surgery. Good! I hoped some time off might help calm him down.

CHAPTER 19

Things That Go Bump In The Night

Steve Moore had been my best friend in high school and college. We had played basketball together, caroused together, come of age together.

Later Barbara and I began our career-driven odyssey — Cincinnati to Columbus (Ohio) to Cincinnati to San Francisco to Baltimore to Phoenix.

Meanwhile, Steve and Janet — the wife-to-be he had met in college when friends bet him he couldn't get a date with a "nice" girl — never left Cincinnati. They lived in the same house for 38 years. Steve built a stellar career as the basketball coach at Oak Hills High School, retiring in 1988.

Well, sort of retiring. Basketball was in Steve's blood. In retirement he continued to coach in various youth leagues, particularly those where his sons and grandsons played.

Late in 2001 I received an email from Janet. Steve had agreed to serve as an assistant coach for a new professional basketball team based in Northern Kentucky, just across the Ohio River from Cincinnati.

Ever since the Cincinnati Royals — featuring Oscar Robertson — left town in 1971 to become the Kansas City/Omaha Kings (and later the Sacramento Kings), Cincinnati has been a dry gulch as far as professional basketball is concerned. The interest and the dollars are attracted toward always strong, often powerhouse teams at the University of Cincinnati and crosstown rival Xavier University. It's a tough environment to nurture a professional basketball team. But from time to time some monied sponsorship group decides to go to the well ... and falls in.

Such was the case in 2001. The Kentucky Pro Cats were being formed, Janet Moore said, and would play in the new American Basketball Association. What's more, she wrote, Phoenix would have a team, and the Pro Cats would be coming here to play early in 2002.

Sure enough, I learned that Steve and the Pro Cats would be in town January 26 and 27. We quickly made arrangements. I'd pick him up at the team's hotel on Saturday evening for dinner at our house.

It was the first time we had seen each other in more than a decade. Barbara fixed beef stroganoff and we spent the evening reminiscing, retelling a few of the old war stories ... while, just like old times, Barbara rolled her eyes.

Of course Honeybear, Bebop and Noché were all over Steve, and he loved it. We did the obligatory demo in the backyard. Honeybear, one of the great scent articles dogs, did her usual perfect number. And Bebop was Bebop — spinning and jumping, retrieving like a dog possessed, executing his signals as if his life depended upon them.

Steve was impressed. He'd be more impressed, I told him, when he accompanied us to our Wow Wob Bassackwards Utility Group the next morning to watch some darn fine dogs frolic through the Open and Utility rings.

About nine o'clock we headed back to Steve's hotel, a far cry from our "Dawn Patrol" days when nights of unparalleled debauchery would end at 5 A.M.

Barbara told me later that after the door closed behind us she had cried. "Steve is one of those people who has defined our lives," she told me, "and I knew I'd never see him again."

She was right, Steve died on September 18, 2005, one day shy of 46 years after he had stood at the altar as my best man.

Barbara's response that evening as Steve and I left for his hotel was a far cry from how she viewed him in the beginning. Our reputation for hell-raising had been conveyed to her before we met in "Fat Ray's" wedding. Barbara was the maid of honor, I was the best man. Later Barbara told me the bride had confided, "Look out for the best man."

But on the evening of January 26, 2002, nearly a half century after our hell-raising had yielded to domesticity, we were all tucked in by 10 o'clock. And I was eagerly anticipating our training session at 8 A.M.

Our group, Wow Wob for short, had decided to train at Pierce Park that morning. Phoenix Field and Obedience Club's obedience trial would be held there in four weeks. We'd train there at least a couple of times before the February 23/24 shows. Dogs have a strong sense of place, and there's much to be said for getting them comfortable with the show site, especially when it's in your hometown and you have access to it in advance.

Steve and the Pro Cats were staying in Tempe, a considerable distance from both our house and the practice site. Jill Wallis, a member of our group, lived near the hotel, and I had arranged for her to meet Steve at 7 A.M. and bring him to Wow Wob. Later I would take him to the Fairgrounds Coliseum where the team had scheduled a noon shoot-around.

■ ■ ■

At 3 A.M. I was awakened by something that went bump in the night. I'm sure the bumping blended into my dreams for a while, and it must have taken some time for me to get fully awake, get out of bed and investigate. The noise was coming from the living room. When I turned on the light I saw Bebop bumbling around, banging first into a table, then a couch, then a chair.

By that time Barbara was up, too, also watching. We turned on the outside lights, opened the back door and let the little guy out into our walled backyard. He didn't want to pee or poop. Instead he wandered around, occasionally stopping to study us, clearly trying to figure out who we were.

Earlier that evening, while Steve was there, Bebop had been his usual playful, whirling dervish self. Now, though, he was disoriented and couldn't stop his aimless wandering around. We finally got him into the house and into our bedroom, where our dogs normally sleep. He wandered around in there for another 20 minutes or so, then settled down and went to sleep.

At 5:30 A.M., I called the hotel, had them wake Steve and told him what had happened. Sorry, I said, we'd have to pass on our Wow Wob get-together. Then I called Jill, told her what had happened and asked her not to pick up Steve. During each call I described what had happened, but I had no idea what it meant.

Around seven o'clock I called Apollo Animal Hospital and left a message for the veterinarian on call. It turned out to be Patricia Bennett, and she called back a few minutes later. She listened to my description of the incident, then said, "That sounds like a small seizure." I had no experience with seizures in animals or people, knew nothing about them. Eventually I realized Dr. Bennett was referring to a petit mal seizure. A type of epilepsy featuring attacks of momentary unconsciousness or disorientation without convulsions — as distinguished from gran mal seizures which feature convulsions.

My later experiences with Bebop's seizures led me to believe that in the living room, in the dead of night, while we were sound asleep, my little guy had quietly convulsed. We had awakened just in time to encounter the final (postictal) stage when he regained consciousness and was bumbling around, disoriented.

On Monday morning I took him to Dr. Toben and had him checked. Bebop was fine. That's the thing about canine seizures — when they're over, they're over. No lasting effects. But it had been a disquieting incident. And it had screwed up my first visit in more than a decade with my former best friend.

I hoped the episode had been a fluke.

CHAPTER 20

Bebop Tours Scottsdale

Marilyn Whitmore and I had trained together for several years. First while Honeybear — in on-again, off-again fashion — was making her way toward an OTCH. Now as Bebop, in his joyous, explosive way, was blazing down the same path. At the time, Marilyn had a Sheltie named Mandy who was on the same trajectory.

Marilyn and I had decided to get together on February 5 at WestWorld of Scottsdale, set up a ring and run our dogs through Open and Utility. In a few weeks there would be a cluster of dog shows and obedience trials on WestWorld's huge polo field. Several practice sessions would help our dogs get comfortable in that setting.

WestWorld is a sprawling, bowl-like 120-acre equestrian and special events facility, hosting everything from horse shows to auto auctions, music festivals to polo matches, balloon launchings to dog shows.

While WestWorld is widely recognized for its recreational facilities and events, they are not its primary reason for being. WestWorld is in a flood plain, in the path of the runoff from the McDowell Mountains. All of the park is a flood-detention basin designed to help protect Phoenix, Scottsdale and Paradise Valley from flooding. When heavy rains cause sufficient runoff from the mountains, the flood waters are detained in WestWorld until they can dissipate.

In the 1980s, the City of Scottsdale entered into an agreement with the Federal Bureau of Reclamation to develop the area now known as WestWorld for public recreational use.

At the time of our training get-together, the west end of the park — just inside the main entrance and just off the busy Loop 101 Freeway — was a 19-acre polo field. I've seen that field under water deep enough to sail a catamaran. To the south of the polo field/detention basin is a high, steep ridge, a dike built to prevent the water from flooding the Central Arizona Project Canal, which runs just south of WestWorld.

A half mile east of the polo field, also in the shadow of the dike, were a large covered equidome, 9 additional outdoor horse arenas and 14 horse barns with 672 stalls.

I like to arrive early for practice sessions, walk my dogs and play a little ball. On February 5, I arrived at one o'clock. It was one of those bright, cloudless, pristine late winter days that tell you all you need to know about why every other person you meet here in Arizona is a transplanted Midwesterner.

Honeybear, Bebop and Noché were in the van with me. Bebop would have his "OTCH lesson." Honeybear would frolic through a light workout to keep her sharp for her conquests in the Veterans ring. And Noché would tear around playing ball.

Turning off the Loop 101 access road and into WestWorld, I took the south road, which borders the polo field and runs along the base of the dike. I drove all the way to the east end of the field, swung left to the edge of the grass and stopped.

Driving in, I saw two people playing ball with a German shepherd near the west end of the long, green field. As I parked and prepared for a round of ballplaying, I thought, *Oh, oh, I'd better keep an eye out in case that big dog comes barreling over here.*

I went to the back of my van, rummaged for a large, colorful squeakie ball, opened the side door and let Bebop out. He hit the ground at warp speed, and I threw the ball some 50 feet in front of him.

Just short of the ball, down he went, flailing wildly. At first it seemed he had caught a paw in his collar. But as he lay on the ground with every limb thrashing, every muscle convulsing, I realized what I was seeing. Bebop was in the throes of a violent gran mal seizure. It was 10 days after his strange behavior the night of Steve Moore's visit.

I hadn't seen a seizure before, but I had been told people often bite their tongues during such an attack. So I stuffed my handkerchief into Bebop's mouth. Later, when Dr. Toben heard that, he rolled his eyes and cautioned me never to do that again with a dog. He said he knew of a man who had lost a finger doing that.

Later I was asked how long the violent part of Bebop's seizure (called the ictal stage) had lasted. I guessed a minute or two, but I really had no idea because it seemed to last forever.

Eventually the thrashing stopped. Bebop lay very still on his left side, eyes closed, breathing heavily. I knelt down and stroked him. After a while he opened his eyes, raised his head and looked at me, but there was no sign of recognition.

I better get this dog into the van, I thought. So I stood up, started toward the van, which was only a few yards away, and called, "Bebop!"

He stood up and looked at me again. I saw terror in his eyes, but no sign of recognition. And that's when he took off. He ran about 50 yards, almost to the steep slope of the dike. There he stopped, looked back and barked at me.

All the time I was calling frantically, "Bebop, come! Bebop, come!" To no avail.

Next he turned left and headed east toward the barns. Not good! My heart began to pound. *There's no way I'll catch this dog on foot*, I thought. So I jumped into my van — where Noché and Honeybear were awaiting their turn to play ball — turned the vehicle around and headed in the direction I had seen Bebop running.

Fourteen barns with 672 stalls! Flanked by 10 horse arenas. A mind-boggling number of places for a frightened border collie to seek cover. I spent the next 20 minutes driving around the nearly deserted barns, stopping occasionally to ask an isolated workman, "Have you seen a loose black-and-white dog?" Always the answer was no. An awful dread began to gnaw at my stomach.

Finally I decided driving around the barns was useless, and I headed back toward the polo field. Honeybear was snuggled in her usual spot between the front seats. Noché was fidgeting around, bouncing from the front seat to the rear seat, looking out every window, wondering how soon she'd get to bound across the polo field grass after a tennis ball. She had no clue that she might never see "Mom" again. Nor could she sense the panic that had started to grip me.

When I got back to the field, Marilyn had arrived. We rolled down our windows and I blurted out what had happened. "Oh," Marilyn said, "as I drove in, I thought I saw a border collie up by the bleachers. I remember thinking, *I'll have to tell Willard there's a dog up there that looks like Bebop.*"

She was referring to a small set of temporary bleachers about two-thirds of the way back toward the entrance. About where, as I drove in, I had seen the people with the German shepherd. So in the stress of the moment I discounted what Marilyn told me, certain she had seen the same dog I had seen. In any case, at that moment the 19-acre polo field was empty — except for the ball I had thrown for Bebop, still lying where it had stopped rolling.

"Let's fan out and circle the field," I suggested. "You go one way, I'll go the other."

I drove back along the south road that led to the WestWorld entrance and the busy freeway. On my right, the broad expanse of the polo field. On my left, the steep embankment that protected the canal. Not a living soul, man or beast, anywhere.

Near the entrance I saw the stables for the Scottsdale Mounted Police and a small administration building. *Maybe somebody in here saw him,* I thought. *Maybe they even have him.* No such luck. The door was locked; no one was there.

Halfway up the north road I met Marilyn, and we encountered a WestWorld employee in a golf cart. "Have you seen a border collie, a medium-sized black-and-white dog?" I asked. He hadn't. But he got on his walkie-talkie and put out the alert to the WestWorld employees who were working in far-flung areas of the park.

At that point I called Barbara, a Realtor who at that moment was overseeing a home inspection. "Bebop had a seizure here on the polo field, " I told her. "Then he panicked and ran away."

I asked her to leave, regardless of what she was doing, go home and monitor the phone. "He's wearing his tags," I said. "Someone might find him and call." Then Marilyn and I resumed the search.

That embankment looming on the south side had been bothering me, although at the time I didn't know a canal ran on the other side. Could Bebop have somehow made it through or over the fence that bordered the south road? Could he have scrambled up the hill? And what was on the other side?

To climb the embankment, I first had to make it over the four-foot fence with three strands of barbed wire. Then fight my way up the steep hill, treacherous with loose gravel underfoot. A dirt road ran along the top.

From the top of the embankment the world was serene. Classic February Arizona, crisp and cloudless. Below, the canal flowed quietly … and did so beyond a no-nonsense chain-link fence. *Well, at least my little guy couldn't have fallen into the canal,* I thought. Nevertheless, I was terrified to the point of nausea. "Stay calm," I told myself out loud, "otherwise you'll blow the whole thing."

The dike stretches a mile and a quarter along the south edge of WestWorld. Starting at opposite ends, Marilyn and I worked our way to the middle. "Did you see anything?" we asked in unison as we met. But the answer was no. Bebop had vanished from the face of the earth.

So we half scrambled, half slid back down the embankment, then gingerly climbed back over the barbed wire fence.

Now what?

From where we stood, we could see the entire polo field. It was deserted. No people, no dog. No sense in recruising that area. So we got back into our vehicles to drive among the barns and arenas again — somewhat aimlessly now. It was beginning to sink in at the most visceral level: I might never see my little guy again.

Somewhere near the most distant group of barns and sometime around three o'clock my cell phone rang. Only Barbara had that number.

"Yes?!" I shouted.

"Go to target," she said. And I cut her off.

"What's target?" I screamed.

"Target, the store," she said. "They have him there."

"Which Target?! Where?!"

"The Target at Frank Lloyd Wright Boulevard and Pima Road, just off the 101 Freeway. When I got home, they had left a message on your phone. It told me to call them back when I know you're coming. Go to the side door near the back. They'll meet you there."

Oh my God!

Frank Lloyd Wright Boulevard and Pima Road form one of the busiest intersections in Scottsdale. What's more, there's a freeway exit there; it pours traffic into the intersection. Cars and trucks going all directions. Nearly 70,000 vehicles pass through that intersection each day.

I must have tracked down Marilyn and told her; I don't remember. But I was out of there in a hurry.

Apparently I had lost track of my fleeing dog right at the point where I jumped into my van, intending to follow him toward the horse barns. The van had been parked facing the polo field, and as I got in, started it and was turning around, I lost sight of Bebop. During those few moments, he must have reversed direction and headed west.

Indeed, the dog Marilyn had seen as she drove in must have been Bebop, running along the polo field toward the main entrance … and the freeway.

To go toward his destination, the Target store, he would have turned left at the WestWorld entrance, then ran south along the frontage road that is the Loop 101 access ramp, against the northbound traffic, about a quarter mile to the intersection of Pima Road, Frank Lloyd Wright Boulevard and the freeway exit and entrance ramps.

I wonder how many drivers braked or swerved to avoid hitting him. I wonder, at the busy intersection, how many Good Samaritans said, "Look at that beautiful black-and-white dog. He's going to get killed." Then got out of their cars and tried to coax my disoriented, frightened border collie to safety. To no avail.

Somehow, by the grace of God, Bebop made it through the traffic and headed up the long entrance lane of the shopping center parking lot, another quarter mile. One would guess more kind souls tried to flag him down in the lot.

When I arrived at that lot, I drove to the north side of the store where I saw two young men, one an assistant manager, waiting by the door. That door opened into a back room.

The sight that greeted me still brings tears to my eyes. In the center of the room, standing or kneeling, eight or ten red-shirted Target employees formed a circle. I remember wondering if anyone was up front in the store to assist customers.

Bebop was in the center. In front of him was a little plastic bowl of water, obviously commandeered from a store shelf for the occasion. By the time I arrived, he was lucid. He wagged his tail and came to me.

I stayed only long enough to thank the group profusely and tearfully, and to have them tell me that all four paws were bleeding. Then we were out of there. The next morning I called the assistant manager to again express my gratitude and find out more about the end stage of Bebop's escapade. He told me that a lady had entered the store through the automatic front door. My little guy had walked in with her. Almost immediately the alarm had been broadcast over the in-store walkie-talkie network: "There's a loose dog in the store."

"I mobilized my staff," the assistant manager told me, obviously bursting with pride over his handling of the situation. "I assigned a couple of people to each aisle in the general area where we knew he was."

The aisles in a Target store cover a huge area. And Bebop was a fast, agile border collie. I'll bet it was a merry chase.

"I assigned one of my men to follow him with a mop and bucket," the assistant manager continued. "He was leaving a trail of bloody tracks."

He told me that the odyssey which had begun deep inside WestWorld ended when a shopper slipped her hand gently into Bebop's collar.

"I looked at his tags," the assistant manager said, "and as soon as I called him by name he settled down, began to wag his tail and was happy to go with me."

■ ■ ■

Before I was out of Target's parking lot that fateful afternoon, I called Apollo Animal Hospital, told them briefly what had happened and said, "I'm still in Scottsdale, but I'm bringing him in." I made the trip in record time, about 35 minutes.

Dr. Toben was off that afternoon, but we saw Dr. Robyn Janes. In her chart notes from that afternoon, she wrote that the pads on all four paws "are worn and torn," and she said, "Bebop is very tenderfooted!" She recommended rest, no exercise until his feet were healed. And she told me to soak his paws in warm water with Epsom salts. Meanwhile, she oohed and aahed about how pretty and sweet Bebop is.

Yeah, I thought, *pretty and sweet and epileptic.* The strange events on the night of Steve Moore's visit had, at the time, been only a blip on the radar. But standing in Dr. Janes' examining room on the afternoon that Bebop toured Scottsdale, I knew we had something serious going on.

■ CHAPTER 21 ■

The Seizure Game

The morning after Bebop's strange 3 A.M. episode, when I heard Dr. Bennett say "small seizure," I thought, *This isn't good.* I was aware that border collies are prone to seizures. Beyond that, I was clueless. So I called Helen Phillips, a friend since the early days of Honeybear. Helen is a bottomless well of correct information and insight. Especially about border collies.

Oh yes, Helen had been there, done that. As a matter of fact, presently she was coping with the problem in Split, a young male border collie for whom she had high obedience/agility/herding hopes.

Helen emailed me a ton of information. It was at that point that I became aware of the wealth of information, misinformation and wives' tales available about canine epilepsy.

I ran across an extensive article about seizures and their effects on training and showing canine athletes. It was written by a veterinarian named Lyn Johnson. It appeared in the July/August 2001 issue of *Borderlines,* the magazine of the Border Collie Society of America.

Buried in that article was this statement: "… believe it or not, a full moon really does bring out the seizuring dogs …"

As I began work on this book, I conducted an exhaustive search for Dr. Johnson. I wanted to learn more about her take on full moons and seizures. I could find no trace of her. The

American Veterinary Medical Association had no record of her. No one knows where she came from or where she went. Maybe she vanished one night during a full moon.

At the onset of Bebop's seizures, Dr. Toben suggested I begin keeping a log. Curiously, three of Bebop's first five seizures were either on the night of the full moon or only one night removed. After that the correlation vanished, just like Dr. Johnson. As this book goes to press, the little guy has had 12 seizures. After his fifth seizure, none was anywhere near the time of the full moon.

By the time Bebop and I found ourselves in Dr. Janes' examining room, I had read enough of the literature about treating seizures in dogs to have made up my mind what I *wasn't* going to do.

So much anecdotal stuff on the Internet! So many remedies with no empirical substantiation.

I encountered a plant called *skullcap*, said to be effective in reducing convulsions. Of course, at one time it was considered to be a remedy for rabies. And this comment seemed interesting: "No one is ever sure of the correct dosage."

Or I could try gold bead implants. Available from Fort Knox?

The Natural Remedy Book for Dogs and Cats had a small section on the use of gemstones in the treatment of epilepsy. Including this gem: "Place amethyst in the pet's aura and a large cluster in the room." Uh-huh. And how do I keep those stones in the aura of my little maniac as he tears around his world?

By the time Dr. Janes and I stood over my pretty, sweet, epileptic little guy with bloody paws, I had had enough of everybody's pet herbs and alternative therapies. It was time to shut down the Internet and serious up.

Clearly, it was time for a neurological consult and magnetic resonance imaging (MRI) exam. I wanted to find out what was going on with my Bopster and why. The problem was — and still is — Phoenix and the Valley of the Sun are a veterinary neurology wasteland. There is only one practice in this fifth largest city in the United States devoted exclusively to veterinary neurology.

Therein lies the problem. When you are the only game in town, you may think you can afford to be arrogant or worse.

I had had two bad experiences with that group in the past. And now, as I mentioned those run-ins to credible people in both the obedience and veterinary communities, I began hearing more tales of attitude problems — even allegations of rough treatment of animals — in that practice. All of which underscored my resolve never again to cope with those people, not to expose Bebop to that situation.

But where to take him?

Dr. Janes and her colleagues at Apollo Animal Hospital got their heads together and someone suggested the highly regarded Veterinary Specialty Hospital, then located in Rancho Santa Fe (now in San Diego), California.

Would I be willing to travel that far? In a heartbeat.

Which is how Bebop and I came to find ourselves with Robin Levitski, D.V.M., on February 19, 2002, two weeks after Bebop had toured Scottsdale. Board certified in veterinary internal medicine (neurology), her special interests included management of canine epilepsy.

When I arrived at the clinic, I was given a background sheet that spelled out Dr. Levitski's impressive credentials. Then in walked this "California girl." She appeared to be born for a surfboard, and I found it hard to believe that she could be so accomplished in esoteric-sounding stuff like sophisticated neuroimaging, spinal and intracranial surgery, and electrodiagnostics.

Shortly before noon I left my lucky little guy in her obviously capable hands and departed the clinic delighted with my choice.

Lunch at Pick Up Stix, a bad haircut, a visit to Baskin-Robbins, and six hours later I returned to retrieve Bebop and get a report. He had undergone complete physical and neuro-logical examinations. The results: "unremarkable." Thoracic radiographs and review of previous bloodwork also led to a verdict of "unremarkable."

They had done an MRI of his brain. It revealed no lesions or masses. The diagnosis: late-onset idiopathic epilepsy. Translation: His seizures had started at eight years of age, much later than is usually the case. And *idiopathic* means "we haven't a clue what's causing it."

As soon as you make it known that you have a dog with seizures, you encounter a host of kindred souls who want to share their canine seizure stories. In fact, there's even an exten-sive website devoted to the subject — www.canine-epilepsy-guardian-angels.com.

And every time I mentioned Bebop's seizures to someone who was in the same boat, I heard, "They'll put him on phe-nobarbital." Usually followed by a dissertation about the nasty side effects of the drug and a warning that it would make a zombie out of him.

Which is why I was surprised and pleased when Dr. Levitski prescribed potassium bromide and only potassium bromide. Likewise, that information surprised the host of kindred souls.

Later, Dr. Levitski would explain her choice of medications. "I always start with bromide," she said, "because bromide doesn't have serious side effects." Phenobarbital, she told me, can sup-press bone marrow, has negative effects on the liver, may even lead to liver failure. Dogs on phenobarbital, "drink more, pee more and have a lot of clinical side effects that owners don't like," she said.

So her medication of first choice is always bromide. "If we get the bromide up to the maximum safe dose and the seizures are still occurring, then I'll add in phenobarbital," she concluded.

■ CHAPTER 22 ■

The Last Hurrah

Phoenix Field and Obedience Club's obedience trials were scheduled for Saturday and Sunday, February 23 and 24, at Pierce Park. I had been assured by Dr. Levitski that there was no reason why Bebop should not continue his obedience competition career. And his paws were healed. My little guy was cleared to continue his OTCH quest.

By the spring of 2001, Bebop had spun and frolicked his way to his UDX. Wild but rarely flunking. By the time we walked into the PFOC trial that Saturday morning in 2002, he had 22 UDX legs. He started the fall season in 2001 by picking up OTCH points in each of his first four shows. He now had 16. Not great, but a foothold for his climb.

I had entered him in Open B and Utility B both days, four chances to pick up a few more points.

The southeast corner of Pierce Park, the quadrant where the trials would be held, is adjacent to a large parking lot. It's also bordered on the south by Palm Lane and on the east by 46th Street. If you arrive early enough on show mornings — say 5:45 or so — you can park at the curb, some 50 feet from the rings, and work out of your vehicle.

Normally we don't do that. We set up a tent on the perimeter of the trial site. But PFOC weekend was different. Barbara had to leave town on Sunday on business. She stayed home on Saturday to pack and do some cooking to tide me over the next five days. So I had decided to keep things hassle-free by working out of my van.

I arrived well before 6 A.M., feeling upbeat and brimming with optimism. Pierce Park holds precious memories for me. It was there that Honeybear launched her splendid career with a red ribbon in Novice A. And it was on that same spot — actually the same 50- by 40-foot piece of turf — six years later that Bebop, in only his second time in the Novice B ring, barely missed a perfect score. Both on this same weekend in February. And here we were again on that happy turf.

But all that good karma was overshadowed by an increasingly dark cloud of apprehension. For most of Bebop's obedience career, the constant refrain from judges and those at ringside had been, "What energy!" Or, "What enthusiasm!" Or, "He's so happy and excited."

More and more, though, I was seeing something much darker. Fear. Anxiety. Unquestionably, across the last few months the tenor of his ring antics had changed. It was no longer, "Whoopee! Let's party!" His vocalizations were more shrill, more intense, and recently punctuated by an occasional high-pitched, hysterical bark. And it was becoming harder and harder to call time out on his spinning and jumping long enough to get him into position to begin an exercise.

Remember the skeleton and luge events at the Winter Olympic Games? Where the competitors lie down on those little sleds, then go blazing down that icy chute? How would you like to step in front of that sled and try to stop it? That was me trying to position Bebop to begin the exercises that Saturday morning at PFOC. He spun. He ran in front of me, then behind me. All the while shrieking at the top of his lungs, punctuated by that hysterical, high-pitched bark. And for the first time that shrieking and barking continued *during* the exercises.

Our first ring that morning was Open B. The judge was Bonnie Lee, of Las Vegas, Nevada. The first exercise was the retrieve over the high jump. I stepped into position about 13 feet behind the jump and said, "Place!" — my command for Bebop to come to my left side, sit by my left leg and be ready. He came around my left side, touched his butt down (forged) for a second, then spun out and began to jump and shriek and bark again. Judge Lee waited patiently while we repeated the scenario a couple more times. Finally I got him momentarily planted in the general vicinity of my left leg — certainly not in heel position by any judge's most liberal definition.

When I threw the dumbbell, it skipped under the ring gate at the far end of the ring. "Relax your dog," Judge Lee said, and she went to retrieve the errant dumbbell. As she returned and was handing it to me for a retoss, she said in a near whisper, "Get your dog in heel position first."

My answer was, "I can't." Looking back, that admission was the lowest point in Bebop's obedience competition career.

Know what? He didn't fail an exercise in that Open B ring. Shrieking and barking constantly, he qualified with a score of 184.5. Five of those deducted points were for my inability to control my dog. I thought that was generous of the judge; I would have taken off at least 10, maybe even excused us from the ring.

Later that morning we entered the Utility B ring of Judge Roland Speck, from Iowa. Same performance: the shrieking, the hysterical barking. But Judge Speck saw it differently. He perceived it as so many had been assessing Bebop's antics for the past several years. In the middle of our Utility B run, between exercises, the judge said, "Such enthusiasm!"

Again, Bebop managed to pass every exercise and qualified with a 187.5, his 23rd UDX leg.

I doubt that anyone at ringside that morning had ever seen anything like it. Later I would describe Bebop's mental state in those rings as "hysterical." My closest training buddy is Alice Blazer, a veterinarian. The person who early in Bebop's career said, "I've never seen him make a mistake." She was at ringside that morning, and her descriptive word was "frantic." Debby said, "It sure looked like anxiety to me."

Right. It wasn't enthusiasm. It wasn't excitement. Bebop had entered a world of emotional hurt in the obedience competition rings. His out-of-control behavior emanated from a terrible fear of being wrong. And he could no longer handle it. He was frantic to the point of being out of his mind.

That morning's train wreck had been neither sudden, random nor unexpected. The runaway locomotive had been hurtling down the tracks, gathering speed, for several years. We had gotten through our UDX and had a foothold on our OTCH quest solely as a result of Bebop's brilliance and athletic prowess. His every ring appearance for several years had been a hair-raising adventure.

And it hurt. This was the little guy I had searched two years to find. The little guy who had barely missed a 200 the second time he walked into the Novice B ring. The little guy who won a Dog World Award in Novice, then missed another in Open when he whined his way through the long sit enroute to his third leg (the sound of things to come, as it turned out).

Brilliant, fast, accurate, this was the little guy of whom I had said, "This is gonna be my Super Dog." The little guy who underwent installation of the Zurich Cementless Total Hip … and came back to jump like a deer. The little guy who had cataracts removed and intraocular lenses implanted … and came back to see like a hawk. The little guy who had valley fever for 14 months and never missed a training session or a trial. The kamikaze dog who plays ball with such intensity that several times he has crashed and burned and had to go on the disabled list for days or weeks with soft-tissue injuries.

But this was also the little guy who turned out to be lacking a circuit breaker that would have kept his emotions from spiraling out of control during competition.

There has never been a second in his life when Bebop hasn't tried his gut-splitting hardest. Too hard. His problems stemmed from a work ethic run amok.

Those were the thoughts that tumbled through my mind as we stood in Rollie Speck's Utility B ring that morning and waited to accept our green qualifying ribbon.

As we walked toward the van following the presentation of ribbons, I knew that morning had been Bebop's last hurrah, his last time in an obedience trial.

How, I asked myself, could anyone rationalize taking a seizure-prone dog into a situation that wound him up that much? In my mind, that would be tantamount to dog abuse.

Bebop was retired. On the day I retired him, we were the 11th ranked border collie obedience team in the United States.

■ CHAPTER 23 ■

A Noble Experiment

Bebop may have been retired, but that didn't mean he'd be relegated to couch potato status. Long before I carried him into our home for the first time, I had been indoctrinated with the facts of life about border collies: "You better have the time to give your BC plenty of work and exercise." And, "A border collie has to have a job."

Border collies without work, without exercise, could be plenty difficult to live with. They'd find their own outlets, and those activities could involve destructive behavior, even aggression.

Bebop had had a job. He had loved it (too much?) and he'd been good at it. But now he couldn't do that anymore, and it was time to move on.

I decided to see how he'd fare in tracking. A friend, Erik Hoyer, a man who had put multiple tracking titles on dogs, took us out in the desert a few times and got us started.

I was shocked. Bebop's behavior in tracking was 180 degrees different from his hyper performance in obedience. He went to the starting line calmly and quietly and went to work. And he got quite good at tracking, too.

We tracked intermittently for nearly four months. *Intermittently* because, while my little guy was the picture of composure as he followed the track, he found a way to be the Bebop I had come to know so well after he found the glove (the object for which he was searching). His reward for finding the glove was to be allowed to play with it. I'd throw it and he'd tear after it and retrieve it. Then we'd play — I'd hold it and he'd tug like a maniac.

Then he'd come up lame. We'd walk back to the starting point with Bebop limping all the way.

Later we learned that my accident-prone, injury-prone dog was having chronic problems with a small cartilaginous bone called the fabella in his left hind leg. What it boiled down to was that every time Bebop cut loose and had a blast, the fabella became inflamed and he limped for a few days.

So we'd track for a few days, then Bebop would be laid up for a few days, then we'd track for a few days ...

All of which came to a halt on May 28 when I had surgery at Mayo Clinic Scottsdale to straighten a couple of toes. Then I was laid up for a few weeks. And it was during that period when all of us were couch potatoes that I was able to step back mentally and view the situation in a different light.

There had never been any question that Bebop had loved to work with me in obedience training and competition. Since his retirement in February, he had been giving me all sorts of signals that he desperately wanted to practice and be in the ring with me. At the time, 13-year-old Honeybear was storming through her spectacular Veterans career, knocking off 198s right and left. What a blessing her second career was! Bebop's career had ended abruptly. I had no puppy coming up behind him, no dog to step into his place. HB bridged that gap. We were still at the shows, albeit in the nonregular classes. I was still in my element, still with my best friends, all of whom I had met and gotten close to through my involvement in dog obedience competition.

Honeybear had come through again.

Several times a week HB and I would go to the park for a light run-through. She loved it and I cherished every moment that old white face was at my side.

So what was I supposed to do, leave Bebop sitting there, expectantly tapping one paw, ready to come out of his coat as HB and I disappeared out the door? He knew darn well we were going to the park to train.

Of course not! When HB and I went, Bebop went — it had been his life.

When we'd get to the park, the very turf where Bebop had run and jumped and spun and learned to be a UDX2 dog, HB and I would get out and do all the things that had been so tightly woven into the fabric of my little guy's life.

And Bebop would sit in the van, watch us through the window and cry as if his heart was breaking. Which it was. Eventually he'd lie down on the seat so he couldn't see. Because he couldn't stand to see anymore.

But he could hear. I'd get ready to start an exercise with HB, and I'd say something like, "Heelwork, Honeybear, heelwork!" Or, "This is the recall, HB!" And a mournful shriek would emanate from the van.

All of which was breaking my heart as badly as it was breaking his.

When Honeybear and I were finished, I'd bring Bebop out to do a few light, no-pressure exercises: a little heeling, maybe a few dumbbell retrieves. Sometimes we'd just play ball. Bebop would be beside himself with joy: flipping, spinning, running in tight circles around me.

What a shame! What a shame! What a shame! I'd think. *He wants so badly to do this. But when we get in the ring he comes unglued.*

While I was out of commission, hobbling around in a special shoe, those thoughts took a new turn. Was there even a remote chance that Bebop's predisposition to implode when the stakes got high could be deconditioned? I knew that the behavior modification program necessary to accomplish that was well beyond my level of expertise. And over the past year we had tried just about every calming medication known to either Western or Eastern medicine: Valium, Rescue Remedy, Clomicalm, Miltown — the list went on and on. All to no avail. In fact, some of them had just the opposite effect, sending him right through the roof.

What we hadn't tried was a really good canine behaviorist. Not that I was deluding myself. Not for one minute. The odds of succeeding, I knew, approximated those of winning the lottery. Nevertheless, Bebop's most defining characteristic had always been his second-to-none work ethic. And again I felt compelled to try as hard for him as he had for me.

But where to go? Who to enlist to help me? The world of animal behaviorists is teeming with clueless quacks. Here in Arizona, to qualify as a so-called "behaviorist," you need the funds to procure a shingle to hang out. Bingo! You're in business. I wanted someone with credentials up the swazoo. A board-certified veterinary behaviorist would fill the bill.

For starters, there wasn't one in Arizona. Here we go again.

Chuck Toben and I talked about it. One of the most highly regarded veterinary behaviorists in the United States, he told me, was Bonnie Beaver at Texas A&M University, College Station, Texas. A mere 1,137 miles from Phoenix, near the Louisiana border. Oh God! But why not? Again I thought, *Why not do the best I can for a dog who gives his best every moment of his life?*

When I called to make an appointment, however, I was told that I would not necessarily see Dr. Beaver. She rarely sees patients anymore. She devotes her time to research, teaching and presumably traipsing around the country "giving papers" at veterinary conferences (and collecting honorariums!). Bebop and I would, instead, be seen by one of her residents. Of course, the voice on the other end of the phone hastened to assure me, Dr. Beaver would be supervising the whole thing ... presumably from Timbuktu.

Yeah, right. Like I'm going to make a 2,200-mile round trip and never lay eyes on the specialist who had motivated the trip in the first place.

Then there was Deb Horwitz, D.V.M., in Bridgeton, Missouri, a short 1,500-mile drive. I called. She was booked solid until sometime in, let's see, the next millennium.

Finally there was Dr. Benjamin Hart at the University of California, Davis. Well regarded, been there forever. He actually came to the phone and talked to me at length. Nice guy, not in any way full of himself. And UC Davis was only a piddling 762 miles away. Well, maybe.

While I was pondering that, I learned that the California Veterinary Medical Association publishes a directory of specialists. They faxed me the listing of behaviorists. Lo and behold, there was a board-certified veterinary behaviorist at the Veterinary Specialty Hospital in Rancho Santa Fe, the very facility where I had taken the Bopster for his neurological workup ... and had a totally satisfactory experience. Patrick Melese, D.V.M., was a diplomate of the American College of Veterinary Behaviorists. I had hit pay dirt.

Just to be certain, I called Robin Levitski, the neurologist who had examined Bebop. Dr. Melese had recently left the clinic, she told me, and had gone into private practice in San Diego. She had worked with him on a lot of cases, she said, and she thought he did a very good job. She gave me his new address and phone number. She ended the conversation with, "If my cat had a problem, I would definitely go to Dr. Melese."

Good enough.

I contacted him immediately. He told me it would be helpful if, before we met in person, I could create a videotape of Bebop in action, showing his behavior in the obedience ring. There were no shows or matches coming up — we were in the depths of our brutal Arizona summer. But our Wow Wob Bassackwards Utility Group challenged summer with: "Damn the heat! Full speed ahead!" And every Sunday morning dawn found us out there doing ring run-throughs. Barbara taped Bebop's run-throughs in the Open and Utility rings. His antics weren't at show intensity and he was rusty, but he cut loose enough to give Dr. Melese the picture.

I sent the behaviorist the videotape with a four-page cover letter detailing the history of the problem. One paragraph in that letter summed it up.

> *There is a hierarchy of winding up situations here. In the backyard — when, for instance, we're practicing scent discrimination — he vocalizes a little bit. When we practice in a park, a bit more. At a fun match (very informal), a bit more. At a sanctioned match (more formal, more regimented), even more. At an AKC obedience trial, where there are a zillion cues — lots of people and dogs, tents, crates, a judge with a clipboard, a stewards' table at the ring entrance, a PA system, etc. — I believe Bebop says, "Oh my god! This is the real thing. What if I screw up?" And he winds up — without a circuit breaker to keep him from going right over the top.*

I closed my letter by asking Dr. Melese whether he thought it would be prudent for me to bring Bebop there for a consultation. Or would it be pie in the sky? He replied affirmatively and we scheduled an appointment in San Diego for Wednesday, July 31.

Dr. Toben found all this interesting, but he was unable to conceal a certain amount of skepticism. When he learned of our appointment, he smiled and said, "You're my guinea pig, Willard."

Six days before we were to leave for San Diego, Bebop had one more seizure, his fifth and the most severe I had observed. We were watching the Arizona Diamondbacks/Colorado Rockies baseball game on television. Bebop was lying on the tile floor outside the bedroom door. I heard him begin to thrash. His convulsions were violent. For the first time, he urinated on the floor during a seizure. Throughout the two-minute episode he snapped his teeth at nothing. Near the end he frothed at the mouth.

During the recovery period, he was disoriented, clumsy, stumbling, hyperactive, then frantic for food. (I didn't feed him.) It took him about a half hour to settle down. The rest of the night was uneventful, and he was fine the next morning.

■ ■ ■

On a sunny, balmy, perfect San Diego summer morning, Bebop and I spent three hours with "Dr. Pat," as he liked to be called. Tall and lean with brown hair, he was quiet, a bit reserved. It was appropriate that the session was about reining in Bebop's hyperness, for Dr. Melese was, himself, a calming presence.

The tone of the morning was a curious mix, relaxed but at the same time intense. No stone was left unturned. My only regret was that I hadn't brought a tape recorder. Across my years of interviewing and writing, I had found my tape recorders to be my most valuable tools (read *security blankets*). I find it hard to participate and take copious notes at the same time. It's the journalistic equivalent of simultaneously patting your head and rubbing your stomach.

As the session unfolded, Dr. Pat and I developed a plan. But when I got home, my sketchy notes didn't do it justice. Fortunately, Dr. Melese sent me a detailed letter and followed that with an audiotape which I transcribed word for word.

The purpose of the steps I would be taking was to decondition Bebop to the point that he could go into the ring and relax, not freak out. But I perceived another benefit, too. When you get an obedience competition dog to an advanced level of training — and that's where Bebop was; he knew the exercises so well that he could totally lose it in the ring and still qualify on automatic pilot — there's nothing new to teach. At that point in training all you have to do is fix what breaks … put out fires. The part I love most is teaching a biddable dog new things. It had been a long time since I had had something new to teach Bebop.

Now, working on the plan Dr. Pat and I had put together, I had the opportunity to teach Bebop the most important exercise of his life … to relax on command.

During our session, Dr. Melese had likened Bebop's behavior to rage syndromes in certain breeds of dogs. The curve starts to climb, reaches a trigger point, then shoots up, up and away. It's unstoppable at that point. Certainly that analogy described Bebop's out-of-control performance at the PFOC trial.

The goal of the work I was about to undertake with my little guy was to be able to catch his winding up at a point in the curve before it took off and went over the top. To achieve that end, I set about teaching him calming exercises, quieting-down responses to directed-relaxation commands.

We started with a "settle" command — as opposed to his "down" command which I had been using throughout his show career to place him in the long down during the group exercises. "Down!" placed him in a sphinx-like position where he maintained attention and alertness.

The new exercise, "settle," was designed to place him in a down stay where his body tension was low, his tail and ears relaxed — totally calm, no matter what might go on around him. As we embarked on this first stage, I was fortunate to have a dog who was solid on the long down. I can't remember him breaking a sit or a down in competition. Whining, yes; break-ing, no. Even though he was solid, I treated the exercise as if we were starting from scratch. We did the exercise on leash. When he was down the leash was on the ground and my foot was on the leash. I left enough slack so he could shift positions, but not enough that he could comfortably get up. If he tried to get up — which he never did — the leash would "correct" him by reminding him it was more comfortable to stay down than to try to stand.

The idea was I should not say anything or otherwise interact with my dog if he tried to get up. We were at the dawn of intro-ducing a new concept to Bebop: reward is not always associated with being dynamic, intense, even active. What I *did* reward was lying quietly. I did so by slipping him a treat, gently praising and petting him — being ultra-careful that my reward behav-ior was not, itself, a stimulus to get up. The intervals between rewards gradually increased.

Eventually I'd give a special release command, "free dog!" — used only within the context of this behavior modification project.

This phase was a piece of cake for Bebop. He was being show-ered with affection for something he already did so well.

We segued quickly to the next step. Now, instead of just being down, he was in what Dr. Melese called the "C" position, body curled into a C with his chin down and pointing toward his hip. The position he naturally goes into when he settles down on his own. Where his body language says, "I'm here, I'm comfortable and I'm planning to stay for a while."

At first I was baffled about how to get him to assume that position as opposed to the sphinx down or all the way over on his side. Then I realized that he was offering that behavior all the time around the house. I began shaping the position I wanted to get — on command and quickly — by rewarding him when he did it spontaneously. I'd see him lying next to my desk in the C position. I'd drop quietly to my knees, say, "Good settle, good settle," and slip him a treat. All of that was done quietly, gently, so as to avoid stimulating him to break. Then, a few minutes later, I'd repeat it. Eventually, with lots of animation, I'd say, "Free dog!" and he'd pop up.

Before long, my "settle" command produced a down in the C position. Sort of. As we shaped what I wanted, his head position proved to be the most difficult piece to control. At first he'd curl into position, but his head would not go down. He'd be watching me, waiting for his treat. I had been instructed not to physically put that head down where I wanted it. Rather, I was to wait him out, no matter how long it took. Sometimes it took five minutes or more. But eventually down it went, and he got his reward.

Which spawned another problem. When we did this as an exercise, I'd be down on my knees, next to him. As I'd reach in with the treat, he'd lift his head to receive it.

Two weeks after our consultation in San Diego, I had a followup telephone conversation with Dr. Pat. He emphasized the importance of "raising the bar" as we shaped the total relaxation I needed. In order to get the treat, Bebop had to become more and more relaxed, and for longer and longer intervals. And, although lifting his head to receive the treat was acceptable in the beginning, we had to tighten the tolerances to the point where he got the treat without moving a muscle, except to open his mouth when the treat arrived.

To help Bebop be successful, Dr. Melese suggested I position myself so as to get the treat to him quickly, before he had a chance to lift his head. The objective, the behaviorist emphasized, was to convince the dog that he didn't have to *do* anything for that treat except what I wanted him to do … lie down and relax.

It took only a few days more before my "settle" command was producing the perfect picture that Dr. Melese wanted. We increased the amount of time Bebop stayed in the C position. Dr. Melese cautioned that he didn't want him lying there like a loaded gun, anticipating his release.

Our on-demand relaxation training program was to proceed along a "distraction gradient," on an imaginary scale of zero to ten, from less to more distractions. Dr. Melese warned me not to set Bebop up in situations where he wasn't ready.

So we started our work with "settle" and the C position in the solitude of a closed-door room or alone in the backyard. We progressed along the gradient to a room where Barbara and I were watching the Arizona Diamondbacks on television. Then to the kitchen. Then to the park. Then outside the ring at PFOC classes on late spring evenings. Finally, outside the ring at obedience trials. At least that was the plan. The distractions, the stimuli, would get harder and harder. Bebop was to learn that in any environment, as Dr. Melese put it, "all bets are on." A settle is a settle … regardless. We were conditioning him to hold it together and relax around stimuli, theoretically of any magnitude.

The settle in the C position wasn't really about a position, it was about a state of mind. And it wasn't an end unto itself, it was only step one, a platform upon which we began to build the relaxation command.

The command word I chose was "soft." But I took care to say it as "saawft," softly and drawn out. "Make sure your voice, your tone, matches what you're asking Bebop to do," Dr. Melese instructed.

And not only did I want my voice to be saying, "saawft," I wanted to relax myself at the same time, to have my body and my disposition saying the same thing. The objective was for "saawft" to become a tool that I could use to take a hyper, bouncing-off-the-walls, yelping dog and turn him into a figurative dead dog in a settle. And be able to accomplish that as a directed state.

Picture this: Bebop and I are alone in the backyard, in a shady spot. Bebop is curled up in his C position, the picture of relaxed bliss. I'm kneeling beside him, stroking him the length of his body, saying "saawft," the word drawn out to match each stroke. His eyes are closed, but he's not asleep; he's lapping it up.

He's learning to associate that word "saawft" with total relaxation. If I'm successful, somewhere down the road, when he begins to wind up, I'll say the magic word, and regardless of where he is or what position he's in, he'll take it down a few notches on my command.

By late August it appeared to be working, albeit still with fairly low levels of stimuli. But I had seen the potency of Bebop's out-of-control behavior, and in an update to Dr. Melese I said: "I predict that somewhere down the road we're going to hit the wall. The stimuli that are eliciting the problem will become more powerful than the rewards for the calming exercises we are teaching."

Bear in mind that the relaxation exercises were not about curing the seizures. Although, even though I've never been able to get any veterinarian to flat out link the two, there is no doubt in my mind that Bebop's missing circuit breaker is somehow neurologically linked to his gran mal seizures.

He continued to have periodic seizures at intervals of about 44 days.

By early September we had progressed to the point where we were working on "saawft" in the real world. On September 4 I took him to the Monday evening PFOC obedience classes. My plan was to do some light heeling outside the ring, interspersed with calming exercises.

I had stepped up his physical exercise because I reasoned that the more I tired him out the less likely he'd be to wind up. Have you ever tried to tire out a border collie? And in any case, giving him sufficient exercise was difficult in 110-degree weather.

That evening, before classes began, I took advantage of the large, open field and was playing ball with Bebop. On the second ball toss, he chased after it and just as he caught up with it he went down and started to flail. Acting on the most important lesson I had learned from that frightening afternoon when Bebop toured Scottsdale, I went to him and quickly attached his leash.

That seizure was the least intense of the six I had so far witnessed. Afterwards he was scarcely disoriented, and within 15 minutes he seemed fine. Nevertheless, I aborted the evening's plan and took him home. It had been 42 days since his most recent seizure — that mother of all seizures during the Diamondbacks game on July 24.

Twenty-nine days later he had another one, right after we went to bed. It was fairly severe, but he didn't lose control of his bowels or his bladder. He stayed disoriented for 25 or 30 minutes, and he felt bad most of the next day, curled up in a little circle.

I was glad the calming exercises weren't meant to stop the seizures. Of course, the potassium bromide didn't seem to be doing much good, either.

■ ■ ■

Old Pueblo Dog Training Club's obedience trials were coming up on Saturday and Sunday, November 2 and 3. Those trials, in Tucson, were among my favorites. The setting was ideal. Old Pueblo for years had held their trials on the grounds of the Ramada Inn. It was an old hotel, built in the 1950s when land was abundant and dirt cheap. The facility was a sprawling two-story property that wrapped around two large, grassy courtyards. Across the years, we had learned just what room to reserve so that we could walk out of the door of our room, go 50 feet and be in the ring.

I cherished the Old Pueblo show site because on that very turf Honeybear had made a comeback that had launched us on our final drive to her OTCH (*Remembering to Breathe*, Chapter 47).

Bebop and I had been at this relaxation stuff long enough that I was anxious to see what we were accomplishing. So I entered us in Open B and Utility B. We'd do a nice settle with "saawft" a few minutes before ring time and see where it took us. Bebop, at 8½, wasn't getting any younger and it was time to fish or cut bait.

We checked in on a Friday afternoon. Just the right room; the rings were a few yards beyond our big picture window. We did a little heeling, a few jumps, walked slowly around the perimeter of the rings, did relaxation exercises at ringside. I was delighted to be there with my dog and a multitude of old friends.

Saturday morning was beautiful, a perfect day for a dog show. Our ring would start at eight o'clock. At 7:30, Bebop, his favorite ball and I went around the side of our building to one of the many large grassy areas where the show wasn't.

I threw the ball. Bebop tore after it … and went down in a flailing disaster of convulsing limbs and muscles, snapping teeth and frothing mouth. As I was kneeling beside him, putting his leash on, a door opened to our left. A head popped out and said, "Can I help you?" It was the late Barbara Handler. She would be one of our judges that morning and was herself a border collie person.

"Thank you," I said. "I've been through this before." (I was a veteran of canine seizures. Wonderful.)

"Been there, done that," she said and closed the door.

When it was over, I led him back to the room. "What took you so long?" Barbara asked.

"He had a seizure," I replied and burst into tears.

Bebop was clumsy and disoriented for a while, and *ravenously* hungry. Later, while we were out of the room, he stole a bag with maybe 10 Bonz in it out of Honeybear's training bag and ate all of them.

It had been 29 days since his most recent seizure. The gap seemed to be closing.

When I went back outside, the word had spread. Everyone I met expressed sympathy and condolences. One friend asked, "Are you going to wait an hour or so, then show him?"

My answer was a terse, "No!" Nor was I going to wait weeks or months, then show him. That morning's incident was the end of the road for my hard-driving little "Super Dog."

We didn't leave. Honeybear was entered in Veterans both days, and at 13 years of age she was on a roll. With scores of 198 and 198.5, she won the class both days. Good old Honeybear. On a couple of my darkest days she came through … again.

That episode in Tucson was also the end of my noble experiment with behavior modification. During our meeting in San Diego, Dr. Melese had told me that one of his regrets was a lack of feedback from so many of his clients. "I help them develop a program," he said, "they leave and I never hear from them again. I don't learn about outcomes."

Back home on Monday morning, I sent him an email. I told him what had happened and that I was retiring Bebop and ending the relaxation effort. Bebop was plenty relaxed when he didn't have to cope with the world of obedience training and competition. I thanked Dr. Pat for his help, and I closed my note with: "At least this time you're getting to learn the outcome."

■ CHAPTER 24 ■

Simply Perfect!

Bebop continued to have seizures, one on December 8, the next on February 8, both at night after we were settled down and sleeping. The climax came early in April 2003. On April 9 he woke us up by flailing next to the bed. Then he repeated the performance the next night, in less than 24 hours. In my research I had read about cases where dogs had daily seizures, often many in one day. Was that where we were headed?

I talked to Dr. Levitski. When we started Bebop on potassium bromide, the dosage was 2.9 ml. each day. As the seizures continued, she had increased his dosage in small increments. Was the potassium bromide having no effect, or without it would he have had more seizures? There was no way we could know.

Following Bebop's back-to-back episodes of April 9 and 10, Dr. Levitski set the dosage at 4.8 ml. I knew from comments that Dr. Toben and Dr. Levitski had made earlier that potassium bromide can be toxic if given in too great amounts. And although no one said so, I sensed that 4.8 ml. was about as far as we were going to go with that medication alone. I guessed that the next step would be the introduction of phenobarbital with its undesirable side effects.

Then, as if by magic, the seizures stopped. As this book goes to press, it's been 47 months since Bebop had those back-to-back seizures. Dr. Levitski waited a long time, six months, before beginning slowly, cautiously, to step down the dosage. And well that she might. Several times Dr. Toben has told me, "My experience has been that if you get seizures stopped, then they start up again, they are more difficult to stop a second time."

Right now we're on a maintenance dose of 2 ml., and I suspect he'll continue that dosage for the rest of his life.

The cause-and-effect issues here represent a mystery composed of variables that we'll never be able to untangle. Why did my little guy's seizures cease? Was it the increase in medication? Or was it the change in his lifestyle? I have to think both contributed.

After Bebop's episode at the trial put on by Old Pueblo Dog Training Club, everything related to competition was over, done, kaput. And with it the stress associated with competition training and showing.

Nevertheless, Bebop still gets to do many of the things he loves so much.

As I write this, I am training two dogs, showing one.

Cheddar, a wonderful golden retriever, a son of Mike MacDonald's SixPak, the eighth-ranked competition dog of all time, is working on his UDX and OTCH.

Bravo!, a rescue border collie from dynamite lineage, is still a puppy and his training has just begun.

Cheddar, Bravo! and I go to one of several local parks to train nearly every morning. Bebop almost always goes along. When Cheddar, Bravo! and I are finished, Bebop comes leaping and spinning out of the van to play ball, do a little heeling (yes, he still forges and wraps), some signals, and maybe a dumbbell retrieve.

Once a week our training group, the Wow Wob Bassackwards Utility Group, gets together, sets up a ring and does run-throughs. Much to the delight of everyone involved, Bebop gets his turn in the ring, usually Open. Cruising toward his 13th birthday, he's a bit stiff, not as lightning fast as he once was, and occasionally his back legs give out. But he's just as wild.

Not long ago, entering the ring, I took his leash off, he spun once and knocked over 50 feet of ring gates. And recently my little canine lathe completed a career-long effort by severing an "unbreakable" plastic dumbbell.

These days we set the high jump at 10 inches, and his broad jump is two boards, close together. Bebop's rear end is deteriorating, getting weaker. All of which doesn't faze him. He still has a blast. Barbara watches him, beams, shakes her head, and says, "Such a little spirit!"

Watching him one morning recently, Debby — who has been present for the whole melodrama, ever since that first lesson when the little guy thought the go-out dish was "tricky" — said, "Bebop must think he's really doing well; he hasn't been corrected for several years."

Exactly! Now it's just for fun. He can forge, wrap, spin, anticipate, pick his butt up, chomp the dumbbell, and who cares?

As we've cut his potassium bromide back, back, back, his life has remained stress free. The seizures were a function of his central nervous system. So were his bouts of frantic activity, which eventually escalated out of control and ended his career. Somewhere, somehow, in that beautiful black-and-white head his "hyper center" and his "seizure center" are linked. I'd bet my life on it. And sometimes in the past, when the electrical impulses started firing back and forth, the outcomes were ugly.

■ ■ ■

A couple of years ago a friend came up to me at a dog show and wanted to talk about border collies. When I first met this lady she was in obedience with Tuli, a cavalier King Charles spaniel. Tuli got a UD but had a knee problem that did not respond well to surgery. My friend had to retire her.

Meanwhile, she, like I, had watched border collies and had been smitten. One of those border collies was Bebop. She had seen his antics in the ring. And she wanted to know — as have many who have watched his antics across the years — "What's Bebop like to live with?"

I gave her the same answer I have given all the others: "Simply perfect!" Then I expanded. I told her how he lies near me all day, perfectly calm until I push the GO button. Then he's the driven animal that the public sees. I told her how he raised Noché. How nice he was with Squeakie, our old cat. How Cheddar, a brash young puppy, had come into our home when Bebop was eight and in many ways displaced him. And how he and Cheddar are now best friends, play fighting like they're about to kill each other, then snuggling up against each other to take a nap. I told her how the maniac she sees in the ring loves to be cuddled at home. And how my alarm clock most mornings is a border collie tongue licking my face.

I told her about the Bebop no one ever sees. My little enigma in a border collie suit.

> Willard Bailey
> Phoenix, Arizona
> November 24, 2004—June 12, 2006